JAN KNAPPERT

THE A—Z OF AFRICAN PROVERBS

KARNAK HOUSE

The A—Z of African Proverbs
by Jan Knappert

First edition published in Britain 1989
by Karnak House
300 Westbourne Park Road
London W11 1EH, UK

Photosetting by Emset
Design & layout: Karnak House

Cataloguing in Publication Data

   The A—Z of African Proverbs
     1. African proverbs. Anthologies.
     I. Knappert, Jan
     398.9'96

     ISBN 0-907015-39-5

Printed in Great Britain by
Billing and Sons Ltd, Worcester

INTRODUCTION

More than a thousand languages are spoken in Africa; proverbs have been found in every African language studied so far. Of all those thousands of proverbs the present book will offer a selection of the very best, the wisest, the most poetic.

Proverbs are the most important expression of human wisdom and knowledge of nature, psychology and reality for the peoples of Africa. Even amongst the literate peoples of Africa, such as the Zulus, the Yorubas, the Swahili and the Arabs in South, West, East, and North Africa respectively, a proverb is a vital part of the conversation in everyday life. It contains the condensed experience of past generations, couched in flowery language.

The present work contains hundreds of African proverbs, collected in all parts of that vast continent, many by the author himself, many more patiently written down by missionaries and other scholars. The majority of these proverbs is labelled with the name of the country of its provenance; some proverbs are so widely known that they could be categorised as, e.g., "North African". Others are given with the name of the ethnic group or the language where each was recorded. In this way it is hoped the greatest possible variety is achieved and the readers will have a fair impression of the richness of African oral traditions.

These proverbs have been enclassified under headings pertaining to daily life; these categories presented themselves to the author as he was collecting. They are the natural representatives of the spheres of activity and thought in the daily life of the people of Africa. These proverbs are the true expressions of African philosophy. This philosophy is, of course, clad in very different garments by the various peoples as they are constantly at work to give shape to their creative spiritual activity. As a result, a people will reflect upon a different aspect of the same problems of daily life that we are all faced with, such as love and death. It is hoped that his book may contribute to an understanding of the peoples of Africa in the Western world.

Proverbs

Proverbs are short expressions of wit, containing the wisdom of past generations in condensed form, often in rhythmic language, easy to remember and pleasing to hear. The fact that there are many hundreds of English proverbs is, of course, well known in the English-speaking world;[1] similarly we possess collections of Latin and Greek *proverbia*,[2] the wise sayings of the philosophers. Collections of proverbs are available in all the major European languages,[3] and we are aware that there are many proverbs in the major Asian languages such as Arabic,[4] Persian,[5] and Chinese.[6]

Usually proverbs are associated with antiquity; we think of the Biblical *Book of Proverbs* and other collections, such as those of Ancient Babylonia and India.[7]

It has been the privilege of the present writer to make his own collection of proverbs in Africa. It is always an experience to sit down with an old gentleman or the village grandmother, and hear them explain the proverbs of their *ethnic group*, each one a gem of tribal thought, and often a literary beauty.

Many African proverbs require an extensive commentary since they cannot be fully understood without some knowledge of the ethnographic background. This works the other way too: a proverb like "Wisdom is more precious than rubies"[8] would be meaningless to a San living in the desert who possesses no wealth, no luxuries and no ornaments except a few iron beads or plaited bracelets. Only by placing a given proverb in its cultural background can we understand its meaning and in doing so gain some insight into different peoples' ways of life and thinking.

Thus, every proverb requires a little story to explain why the proverb was phrased as it is. For instance, the proverb "Wisdom is more precious than rubies" was intended for princes. The average inhabitant of Solomon's kingdom never saw rubies, but the king's many lazy sons were more interested in jewels than they were in the art of governing the kingdom. This proverb, like most of its kind, was originally meant to be taken literally.

Let us examine two Dama proverbs: "If you have a cup of sweet milk, be content", and "An ugly object may hide something sweet"; both refer to a particular scene from life in the deserts of Namibia (the word Namibia means "desert country"[9]) where a certain gnarled and knotty tree of the *doringboom* type grows. The hard outer bark is layered on the inside with a soft inner bark, a fibrous substance which contains a syrupy liquid, not unlike molasses but sweeter. The Dama love to drink their milk in the shade of this tree; they cut off strips of the bark, dip the inner bark in their milk and then suck it. Sitting around together and drinking this sweet milk is the Dama's chief delight. So the proverb means that no-one should ask for more than to sit in the shade of this ugly tree and drink his sweet milk: the wisdom of being content with simple things. The other proverb arising out of this situation signifies that ugly objects or people may well contain sweetness and goodness.

Nothing is closer to the heart of African society and thought than the proverb. More than any other African tradition, it expresses the essence of African wisdom. Many proverbs are simple and clear in meaning and can be universally applied—we can learn a great deal about human nature from them. For example, the Bambara proverb "Let the tree float in the river. It will never become a crocodile", refers to the kind of person who tries to pass himself off as being powerful and aggressive, whereas in reality he is harmless and passive. Such types can be found among all nations. This, indeed, is the secret of proverbs: they reveal the unity of mankind and the universality of our human emotions, thoughts and problems.

However, many proverbs refer to some aspect of the local culture which the student of proverbs needs to understand. Since each nation has its particular attitude towards life, each expresses its experience of life in its own unique words. For instance, the Swahili, an old civilised nation who follow Islam,[10] see this life as a preparation for the next: "Happiness is obeying God's will, for following His law will open the gate of Paradise". Other African peoples have a very different idea of happiness. In Mozambique they say, "The frog is happy with his numerous offspring''; in Tanzania, "Happiness is to have peace, shade and no hunger".

The present writer's long experience in Africa has shown him that all men pursue essentially the same purposes, have the same basic desires and fears, and feel the same pains whether caused by hunger or by love. Another common experience is good and bad luck, with the feeling that it is always someone else who has the good, and onself who has the bad luck. So, while the feelings are the same the world over, the way that different peoples express these differ, although the meanings may well overlap. For instance, in Swahili the word "love" can also mean "will", and "hate" also means "disgust". In Lingala the word for "intelligence", "wisdom", also means "cunning". In Alur the verb "to propose to a girl" is the same as "to talk eloquently". After some reflection, the logic of the associations between these words will become evident. In this way the African proverb has much to teach us about human nature and the way we think.

There are other common links between ideas and experiences in many parts of Africa: in East Africa, for example, "The poor man's boat sinks", and "The poor man's hens never lay eggs", indicate the association between poverty and bad luck. But is the poor man poor because he is "magically laden" with ill luck as the result of being "ill-starred", or simply because he is unable to buy healthy hens and a good boat? One North African fable provides an answer: the only farmer whose hens were not stolen by the jackal was the one who sat up all night and shot the beast. "The vigilant farmer keeps his fowl" is the proverb which accompanies the tale.

Similarly, poverty is associated with loneliness. This too is explicable in two ways: the poor man is shunned by everybody since no one wants to share his misery or be friendly with a man who always fails. Conversely, I was told that poverty is also the *result* of loneliness—a man with plenty of brothers, friends and relatives will never go hungry, whereas a man on his own is likely to be beaten up and robbed if he has no one to call on for help.

Wisdom in Africa is invariably linked with survival. There are innumerable fables about the wily weasel, Kabundi, about Kobe the clever tortoise, Sungura the crafty hare of Tanzania, and many other intelligent animals who survive by their wits. In Africa there are many more dangers and enemies surrounding one than in Europe or America, and the survival of the wisest is a major theme throughout African folklore. The stupid donkey is the one who always gets the blame and the beating, while the wise monkey has already disappeared with the food. Either you resort to trickery or you starve, is the philosophy of many African peoples who live in a harsh environment where lack of food is a daily problem.

The whole rich spectrum of human experience—the love of parents and children, the problems of courtship, the luck of the hunter, the adventures of the traveller, the dreams of the lazy and the scheming of the ambitious—is to be found in African proverbs.

So far as we know, there are proverbs in all African languages and dialects, but since not all these have yet been given a written form, we cannot make any absolute statement. We can begin to understand how proverbs came into being by reading the books of some of the experts, for example, Dr. Vedder's work on the Bergdama[11] One can even witness the birth of a proverb, for sometimes the person who invented it is remembered as well as the situation which provoked it. Such expressions are often changed over the generations, losing their original meaning and gaining different overtones.

Among the Swahili,[12] the proverb-maker has to be a poet; his new proverb must have a rhythm and ideally a rhyme too. Thus many proverbs are fixed into one or two lines of very fine verse.

Amongst the Yoruba, however, no one is allowed to make new proverbs. There is a known set of true proverbs which only the elders have the authority to pronounce. The young are only permitted to use imitation proverbs, and if any young man does happen to use a proverbial expression in the presence of an elder, he has to apologise by saying, "It looks like a proverb but it isn't a real one!" The polite answer to that is, "May you live to quote real proverbs!"[13] In spite of this extreme conservatism and exclusivism, evolution cannot be checked, least of all in an oral tradition. Like songs, proverbs do change in content, form and number. Each generation can create its own classics, which is impossible in a written tradition. The function of proverbs in some African societies is so fundamental that one might say that no negotiations of any kind could take place without them. An example of the proverb in Swahili "In the lion's footsteps no man should walk", is given in my *Bantu Myths and other Tales*.[14] There the function of proverbs was to save the king's face as well as the interests of his wise counsellors.

In this author's own case proverbs were used by his mother as an educative device, but in Africa proverbs may also be used by the younger generation to address their elders. There, unlike Europe, grey hairs are still respected, and no young person would dream of telling an older person what he ought to do, for, as the proverb says, "Does the chick teach the hen to scratch?" This proverb, or one of its variants, is almost universal in Africa. In Angola, to argue their case, children might say to their father, "The sun does not change but the clouds do", meaning that the sons will be different from their father, who, by implication, is flatteringly compared to the sun.

Proverbs, like fables, have a message for the listener; they are also intended to pass on the lore and morality of the local culture to the younger generation. We have only to think of the common proverb "Honour thy father and thy mother" from the Bible (Exodus 20:12) which is found all over Africa.

African proverbs are often couched in the form of a question, to make them sound more gentle, e.g., a variant of the proverb given above is "Does the cub teach the lion to hunt?" Such a proverb might be used by a parent whose child is cheeky; it puts him in his place without using hard words. From my own childhood experience I know how effective this was as a way of upbringing. For instance, when there was a dish to be divided, we children would each shout, "Me first!" Our mother would reply, "First the donkeys, then the long-ears". Puzzled, we would pause, wondering what she meant, until it dawned on our young minds that long-ears were the same as donkeys, and that we ought to wait quietly until we were each given our share. Human children ought not to behave like young donkeys. The proverb can only function in a culture where the word donkey is associated with stupidity.

Adults as well as children have to be "cut down to size" from time to time, both by their equals and by the young. "The dove will feed his young as well as himself" is an obvious proverb to be used in the presence of a greedy parent by hungry children.

Teaching is not the only function of proverbs—they may also be used as a form of consolation for someone who is suffering. "Children have a duty to look after their old mother" may be a statement of an accepted rule in the community, but it may also be used to comfort a woman in labour: "Now the child causes you pain, but later he will take care of you". Even a pair of seemingly contradictory proverbs like "After rain comes the sunshine", and "After sunshine comes the rain", can both be used to console someone who has known happiness in the past, and to one who is at present suffering. A proverb like "Many hands make light work", or, as the Swahili say, "One man cannot launch a ship", is contradicted by "Too many cooks spoil the broth", or, as they say in Bambara, "Ten tailors will never finish one garment". The answer to this problem is, of course, that the proverbs can be used in different work situations, that for each type of work the right number of hands is needed, neither more nor less. The purpose of the proverb is not a fixed function in every recurrent identical situation. Proverbs are flexible parts of human understanding of this world, ready to be adapted and applied to suit a particular, unique situation. Like people, proverbs have to function in an ever-changing unpredictable world, or be lost.

Contradiction in proverbs has long exercised students of folklore, because they study the words of the proverb rather than its purpose. Proverbs have a three-tiered meaning, quite apart from their many ramifications in daily usage. For instance, the proverb "No fruit falls far from the tree" describes a fact already observed by Newton, and proverbs are obviously not intended to describe physical facts. Proverbs

8

are intended for people; they are about people. The users of this proverb will explain that it represents the relationship between parents ("trees") and children ("fruits"). Just as an apple tree can only produce apples, so apples can only grow on apple trees. Does the same apply to human families? An expert in heredity may deny that all sons resemble their fathers, but again that is not the purpose of the proverb. It tells us what we have to believe in. The son is *expected* to resemble the father, to "follow in his father's footsteps". "No greater joy for a good father than a son who is like him." The son can do no better than to imitate his father. If that is the rule, society will be preserved by the efforts of its members to conform; and continuity is the aim of every society. It is like a living tissue that keeps its component cells alive as long as they are willing to live inside it. The proverbs are the tools by means of which its members are kept in line. The same proverb is also used conversely to keep the father in line, as it implies that a poisonous fruit can only be the product of a thoroughly evil tree. The very fear of perverting his son by his bad example will induce the father to observe the laws of his society. The son's guilt is thrown onto the father—bad fruits grow on a useless tree. It is an age-old association between an abundance of healthy fruit and the morality of fertile households. Thus the study of proverbs becomes an exploration into the implications of social intercourse, the moral rules that are hidden in simple, common sentences, so that eventually the persistent student of a people's proverbs will understand both their language and their culture.

"A wise man who knows proverbs can settle disputes",[15] says the Yoruba proverb. Among the Yoruba, as among many other peoples of Africa, the knowledge of proverbs is a vital instrument for what one in America would call "making friends and influencing people". The proverb prepares young men for their careers as heads of families, clans and villages. They will use proverbs as instruments of peace, impressing the contending parties with their wisdom, so that they may cease their hatred. Proverbs relating to these matters have been arranged in this work under the headings of "leadership", "war and peace", "society", "experience", and several others, for proverbs often have multiple uses.

It will be seen that each heading provides the rubric, the social context in which a proverb functions. More rubrics could have been found, but I trust that most of the essential categories are represented. These categories are the fields of human thought and activity in which the proverbs operate, the situations in which a particular set of proverbs might effectively be "hurled like the stone that scatters the dogs".

The smallest unit in every society is the family, and many proverbs refer to (one might say "regulate") the relations between parents and children. Some categories of people are more expressly the "target" of proverbs than others. Sons and daughters, wives, nubile girls, neighbours, chiefs and elders, fools and sages, hunters, fishermen and farmers are the most prominent proverb personalities.

Certain feelings and states of mind are frequently mentioned in proverbs, such as love and hate, rancour and forgiveness, friendship and enmity, happiness and sadness. Man's physical conditions include poverty and wealth, blindness, illness and fatigue. The normal activities of human beings are: working, eating, drinking, sleeping, travelling, talking, resting and dying. The stages of life are, of course, vital: birth, youth, marriage, parenthood, old age and the approach of death. The full spectrum of human life is thus reflected in proverbs. Indeed, some elderly people in Africa have assured me that there was no aspect of life about which they could not quote a proverb. Proverbs are part of life.

The reader would therefore do well to keep in mind the category in which the proverb he is reading belongs, as this will give the clue to its meaning. For instance, there is a proverb from the Tsonga nation in Transvaal: "When you see a fly, it comes from the dirt"; this has been placed under the heading "Good and Evil". Since "dirt" is obviously associated with "evil", and since proverbs are about human beings, not about insects, the subject of this proverb is a human character comparable to an African fly: always eager to alight on sensitive places such as eyes and sores, pretending to be prefectly at home there, then settling on your food and licking that. Such a character is essentially dirty, and has been associated with evil ever since the Devil was called "Lord of the Flies" in the Bible. Thus the heading "evil" links the fly to a human character. Proverbs are poetic commentaries on human life and society. Many proverbs have equivalents in several parts of the world. For instance, "From the frying pan into the fire" is rendered in Holland as "From the rain into the drop", but in East Africa I heard a more poetic expression: "From the lion's claws into the hyena's jaws". This saying does not seem to be a proverb in spite of its ubiquity. Yet it carries an implied advice not to get entangled in such a situation, which it generalises by means of a poetic expression. It can be fitted into a conversation like, "If I did as you tell me to do it would be for me like falling out of the frying pan into the fire", a polite way of refusing, with good reason.

The intention of this book is not to give a complete survey of African proverbs. That would only be possible in an encyclopaedia-sized book. In a small country like Burundi alone, 3,000 proverbs have been recorded.[16] The author's own collection of just Swahili proverbs is approaching the 2,000 mark. It is highly probable that the total number of proverbs circulating in the whole of Africa may surpass one million. It may one day be possible to assemble a more complete anthology of African proverbs than this slender volume which can do no more than whet the appetite of proverb-lovers for the great treasures of African wisdom. This book intends only to prove that the people of Africa do possess original proverbs, very beautiful and very wise ones. May these gems of generations-old sagacity provide enjoyment for many readers in the English-speaking world. Proverbs are made not only for learning, but for pleasure too, and often for a refreshing laugh.

Notes

1. See the magnificent *Oxford Book of English Proverbs* by W.G. Smith.
2. *Adagia sive Proverbia Graecorum,* by Zénobios, n.p., 1612.

11

3. See the bibliography in M. Maloux, *Dictionnaire des Proverbes, Sentences et Maximes*, Paris: Larousse 1960, pp. xiii-xvi.
4. J.L. Burckhardt, *Arabian Proverbs of the Modern Egyptians*, London 1875. Classical Arabic collections by J. Scaliger (1614), S. de Sacy (1826), and G.W. Freitag (1838).
5. *Persian Proverbs* by L.P. Elwell-Sutton, Wisdom of the East Series.
6. H.H. Hart, *700 Chinese Proverbs*, London 1937.
7. A. Blau, *Indische Sprueche*, Leipzig 1893; H.C. d'Errey, *Choix de Proverbes indiens*, Pondichéry 1934; N.R. Haldar, *Collection of Sanskrit Proverbs*, Calcutta 1872; J. Lazarus, *Tamil Proverbs*, Madras 1894.
8. *Proverbs* 3:15.
9. See Knappert, *Namibia, Land and People, Myths and Fables*, Leiden: Brill, 1981.
10. Knappert, *Traditional Swahili Poetry*, Leiden: Brill 1967.
11. Hamburg 1913.
12. See Knappert, *Swahili Proverbs*, University of Cologne 1985.
13. Evan Rowlands, *Teach Yourself Yoruba*.
14. Leiden, Holland: E.J. Brill 1977.
15. J.O. Ajibola, *Owe Yoruba*, London: Oxford University 1955, p.42.
16. F,M. Roodegem, *Sagesse Kirundi*, Tervuren, Belgium 1961.

APPEARANCE

The face is like a riverbank, it looks smooth but
the interior is like a rockface   *Dama*

The snake may change its skin but stays a snake.
It has always two tongues.   *Dama*

An ugly tree may yield sweet sap. (The Nami-
bian *doringboom* yields a sweet juice.)   *Namibia*

Smiling teeth are like an empty ostrich egg.
(Hypocrisy provides food for no one.)   *Namibia*

Some smile with hatred in their hearts.   *Angola*

An ugly girl can bear children just as well as a
pretty one.   *Sudan*

A vulture is a bird but not meat. (Islam forbids
the eating of vultures.)   *Hausa*

If you have white teeth, you may smile.   *South Africa*

Catch soft birds with sweet words.   *South Africa*

The mango shines but has a stone inside it.   *Tanzania*

The beauty of the maizecob may deceive you   *Tetela*

Do not buy a rat in a bag.   *Tetela*

People are like cowdung: hard on the surface,

slippery inside.   *Buganda*

God gives meat even to people with ugly teeth.   *Buganda*

The dog with lovely large eyes may be a good
hunter or a thief.   *Buganda*

A man's knowledge cannot be read in his face,
nor can a woman's virtue.   *Swahili*

If the woman is beautiful she will have many
faults.   *Zigula*

The most evil satan will look like the most
attractive woman.   *Swahili*

The lover sees the smoothness of the woman's
skin. The doctor sees the illness hidden under it.   *North Africa*

The tree with the sweetest fruits is guarded by
the demons.   *Nkundo Zaire*

BEGGARS

We are all beggars at His door.	*Swahili*
A beggar who has got a job will do it carefully lest he has to appeal again to people's pity.	*Kimbundu*
The chimpanzee will have to live without a tail.	*Congo*
Abundance of dung will attract flies	*Swahili*
Some people are like thorn bushes: if you come near them they catch hold of you and won't let you go.	*Hausa*
Give a beggar a finger, he will take the whole hand.	*South Africa*
If a beggar has chickens, they will not lay.	*Swahili*
Teach him begging and he will be first at the gate of the great mosque.	*Egypt*
The crow does not overlook meat drying in the sun.	*Kwanyama*
The fisherman hides his fish from the beggars.	*Kenya* *Namibia*
One who cooks his own food does not beg.	*Kikuyu*
Laziness is soon overtaken by poverty	*Kikuyu*

15

When the lion is ill, the mosquito does the cupping. (Parasiting on a weak body.)   *Buganda*

If you only sleep you will be hungry. If you only pray to God you will be hungry. You will have to put in hard work.   *Congo*

Beggars will not lick a bleeding hand. They will lick a hand covered in palm-oil.   *Yoruba*

Money does not grow on my back (Said to one who asks for money.)   *South Africa*

If you had not given food to beggars you would have eaten it yourself (In time of famine we all starve anyway.)   *Zambia*

The jackal persuaded the hyena to beg some meat from the lion.   *Namibia*

The poor man's boat always sinks. He gets fish by begging.   *Swahili*

One day you will have to beg God for mercy. Be mercyful to beggars now.   *Morocco*

The elephant eats with his two cheeks full of food, the rat with only one.   *Congo*

We all love money, but money loves only some of us.   *Congo*

Ants surround the dying elephant.   *Zaire*

THE BLIND

A blind man does not say:	*Yaunde*
I will fling a stone. How could he hit?	*Cameroun*
It is easy to make a blind man jump: Shout at him that there is a snake near his feet.	*Nigeria*
Your friend will weep for you even if he is blind ·	*Burundi*
A blind man may hear more than you see.	*South Africa*
If you are blind, do not pick up a stick: it may be a snake.	*Sudan*
A blind man may see with the eye of the soul.	*Swahili*
Let them pull me, let them take me, said the blind man when he heard them beat his mother.	*Hausa*
If you eat from a blind man's plate, make sure you do not touch his fingers. (If you take a man's wife as your paramour, make sure he will never know.)	*Swahili*
People will run into the nettles with open eyes.	*Buganda*
The eye is not a thing that one can ask for.	*Kikuyu*
A blind wife will be faithful.	*Swahili*

A blind man will not covet the tempting glitter
of this world. *Morocco*

If God wishes a man to go astray,
He will make his heart blind. *Swahili*

A blind man does not see women's ornaments.
Yet he may beget children with good eyes. *Morocco*

The blind man does not fall into the well.
He knows how to avoid it. *Morocco*

The proud king was made a blind beggar by
God. *Swahili*

Even a blind man can know the price of a lamb. *Egypt*

The man in love is blind. The woman in love
has her eyes half open. *Zaire*

Your eyes are worth a fortune. Save them. *South Africa*

BUSINESS

When the termite hill rustles, go get your
basket.   *Yaunde*
(Termites are collected as a delicacy when the
swarming season begins. Be ready when the
time is favourable.)

When you want to sell a cow you have to leave
home.   *Angola*

You cannot reproach the bedbug that it stinks
after you crushed it.   *Angola*
(You cannot reproach the owner for suing you
after you damaged his property.)

A good sell is a joy for a good salesman.   *Angola*

A clever businessman borrows ("eats") other
people's money, while hiding his own.   *Angola*

When cat and mouse make an alliance,
shopkeeper watch your wares!   *Egypt*

Don't pat the cow before you milk her.   *Hausa*

No profit without travelling.   *Zaire*

If you keep counting the clods you will not
finish the plot.   *Tanzania*

Ten tailors will sew your garment badly.   *Bambara*

Business first, then your girlfriend.	*South Africa*
A coin in cash is better than ten on credit.	*Bambara*
A merchant has an eye on his cupboard and an eye on the street.	*Egypt*
Never lend more than you borrow.	*Egypt*
A salesman is as adhesive as a tick.	*Egypt*
In times of famine salesmen mix the corn.	*Libya*
One "here-it-is" is better than ten "you'll get it later".	*Bambara*
Where the vultures.alight, there is the carcass.	*Namibia*

CAUSE AND EFFECT

If you do not buy your wife enough cloth,
her buttocks will be publicly seen.   *Zambia*

When you scratch, your skin will change colour.   *Namibia*

A sticky tree stem will sweat ever more resin.   *Namibia*

Do you want to harvest corn without cultivating
corn?   *Sudan*

If your teeth are turning yellow, blame it on
tobacco juice.
If the dinner was not ready, was the firewood
not wet?
If your handwriting is faulty, blame it on a
useless pen.   *Uganda*

If it has legs it will have a head.   *Tanzania*
(When a calf's legs are born the head will come
too.)

You lit the fire, now the smoke hurts your eyes. *Tetela*

If you turn, your nose will turn too.   *Tetela*

Where cows have grazed you can collect cow
dung.   *Ethiopia*

If you work like a slave you will eat like a king. *Ethiopia*

If you want to get rid of the flies, throw the
bad meat away.   *Zambia*

The barking of the dogs does not make the
sheep look up.   *Yoruba*

If you have a monkey under your blanket,
it will move and make a bulge.   *South Africa*

The sun dries the lagoon when the tide is out.
The fish will die when it is dry.   *Swahili*

A monkey is an ugly thing, even with a golden
ring.   *South Africa*

Fun is like a young cucumber, if you pick it, it
will wilt.   *South Africa*

Sweetness is only as long as your finger.   *South Africa*

The one who has makes fun of the have nots.   *Uganda*

He shakes his head who does not like strong
drink.   *Zaire*

To sow is to reap. He who excretes on the road
will find flies when he comes back.   *Yoruba*

A good tongue meeting another good tongue
will cause happiness.   *Congo*

If they raise their voices they have trouble. *Congo*

CAUTION

The partridge has to see with its eyes and with
all its feathers as well.   *Yoruba*

The wise man avoids meeting the angry bull.   *Yoruba*

The chameleon looks in all directions before
moving.   *Uganda*

The tortoise carries his roof with him.   *Swahili*

Other people's wisdom often prevents a chief
from being called a fool.   *Yoruba*

Only the mother leopard will carry the young
leopard.   *Kenya*

The leopard you are hunting may circle round
and suddenly run after you.   *Liberia*

When you throw your spear at an elephant
make sure you do not miss.   *Liberia*

For fear of the leopard the goat stays with
people.   *Liberia*

Rats never sleep on the mat of the cat.   *Liberia*

Don't shake the water in the calabash: do not
trouble it.   *Angola*

The mole travels underground, safe from
people's feet.   *Zambia*

A little snake never lies on the path.	*Zambia*
Let your mouth be the trap of your words.	*Zambia*
Hot water does not stay hot forever.	*Congo*
If you meet a snake, kill it outright.	*Swahili*
Where there is moke, there is fire. Where there is fire there are people. Where there are people there are also wicked people.	*Swahili*
When the hare heard the lion he turned and went away.	*Tanzania*
It is easier to find trouble than to avoid it.	*Congo*
Do not put your goat out to graze in the field of the leopards.	*Congo*
Watch the chameleon: it treads ever so carefully, and it can make itself hard to see.	*South Africa*

CHILDREN

Without children the world would come to an
end.   *Swahili*

Children speak only words they have heard.   *Yaunde*

The first-born is fussed over.   *Zambia*

Without children a house is sad and silent.   *Swahili*

Children are no more separable from their
parents than the stripes from the zebra.   *Angola*

When a child has learned to wash his hands
properly he may have dinner with his parents.   *Ghana*

When a child has climbed a tree a little way he
will come down again.   *Ghana*

An only child in a big empty house, have pity.   *Ghana*
(A large family is considered necessary for
happiness.)

A fine cradle will not always ensure a fine
character.   *Ghana*

When you are grown up you can no longer
wear children's clothes but you can still eat
children's food.   *Ghana*
(An adult has adult responsibility but should be
modest and temperate.)

When your child says "I will grasp the fire", let him try it. He will soon throw it away. *Ghana*

The son of a thief must not imitate his father. *Yoruba*

The songs of the old are the laughter of the young. *Uganda*

The ears must never grow above the head. (Children, don't think you are wiser than your parents.) *Tanzania*

Children are dear to the heart and dear to the purse. *South Africa*

When your child pretends to be dying, then you pretend to be making preparations for his funeral. *Ghana*

Do not forbid your son to eat his porridge hot: his burnt tongue will teach him what you can't. *Tetela*

Your son is always better than your brother's son. *Mali*

As you bring your child up, so it will grow up. *Uganda, Swahili*

Without children it is a dead house. *Kenya*

COOPERATION

Hornblowers! Blow in unison!	*Buganda*
One man cannot launch a ship.	*Swahili*
Over many rollers can the ship be moved.	*Swahili*
One man cannot collect the crops.	*Kimbundu, Angola*
You have to ask your friend to help you put the load of firewood on your back.	*Zulu*
Many fishers together will catch even the small fishes.	*Buganda*
Teeth without gaps chew the meat.	*Buganda*
If you are in one boat you have to row together.	*South Africa*
One finger cannot wash your face.	*Congo*
Let the hoes be the same number as the hoers.	*Zulu*
Mr Helper will always come back to do more, even at his own risk.	*Zulu*
Cultivation will never cease.	*Kikuyu*
Only a lonely fool tries to do the work of many.	*Kikuyu*

If the fingers of one hand quarrel, they cannot
pick up the food.   *East Africa*

A numerous family is good for working
but bad when eating time comes.   *Buganda*

The waxbills always fly in pairs.   *Zulu*

We join together to take wise decisions, not
foolish ones.   *Yoruba*

Two strong men will move a heavy stone.
Two bright lawyers will not agree about the
meaning of a word.   *North Africa*

Monkeys pick fruits together.   *Liberia*

Help the hunters, they may give you some meat.   *Zambia*

One arm cannot work.   *Zambia*

Let the singers sing in unison, then the job can
be done.   *Zulu*

Let the elephant fell the trees, let the bushpig
dig the holes, let the mason wasp fill in the
walls, let the giraffe put up the roof, then we'll
have a house.   *Zaire*

Paddle all together, left, right, left, right.   *Zaire*
(Rower's song.)

COURTESY AND MANNERS

Courtesy is the hallmark of education. *Swahili*

A kind person is the one who is king to a
stranger. *Kongo*

Everyone is polite to a chief but a man of manners is polite to everyone. *Kongo*

Diligent is he who works for a sick old man. *Kongo*

A badly brought up boy is as bad as a baboon. *Kunama*

A jumpy guest will eat no chicken. *Buganda*
(A guest has to stay a while and converse before
the host will offer him the traditional chicken.)

A polite mouth can open doors. *South Africa*

Lucky is the man whose son has manners. *Swahili*

Modesty shows good upbringing, but without it
you will be richer. *South Africa*

A gentleman is recognised even in simple
clothes. *Swahili*

The soft voice loosens the gift from the chief's
hands. *Ewe Togo*

The well brought-up man eats with one hand
even when he is hungry. *Ewe*

Humility is the crown of virtue.	*Egypt*
Ingratitude is the worst of sins.	*Egypt*
Honour your grandmother. Without her your mother would not be here.	*Namibia*
The rod will teach the rude son manners.	*East Africa*
Poverty teaches courtesy.	*South Africa*
When he barked I knew he had the character of a dog.	*Swahili*
With your hat in your hand you will travel through the land. (Good manners will open doors.)	*South Africa*

DEATH

What eats you will not jump over you.   *Namibia*
(Death will not forget you.)

The sleeping mat is easily blown away by the
wind.   *Zulu*
(Man dies easily.)

The elephant dies only after all the hunters have
stabbed him.
He is strong like a rock.   *Zulu*

The dead who were buried in shallow graves
will haunt the living.   *Buganda*
(Only close relatives will be buried properly in
deep graves.)

Death is a guzzler: he takes both the fresh beer
and the old.   *Zulu*

The body is earth. When earthenware breaks,
it reverts to earth.   *Ethiopia*

Mourning never rots.   *Mozambique*
(A dear one is never forgotten.)

Enjoy life like food: leave some for your
children.   *Zulu*

The Earth does not grow fat.   *Zulu*
(Even after 'eating' so many people.)

Death gives no warning and no delay. *Swahili*

Many are killed by folly
None are killed by caution. *Yoruba*

Death is like a thief: he never announces his
visit. *Congo*

When the goat looks at his butcher,
do you think he wants to die? *Yoruba*

Death has no preference. *Congo*

In the end the swimmer will be called by the
water. *Zigula*

After the worms have eaten your father they
will eat you. *Nande*

Hunger will kill the last cow. *Liberia*

Disease will wipe out a town sooner than war. *Liberia*

Blood does not dry on the warrior's spears. *Liberia*

For a small death they measure a little grave. *Zambia*

It is the silent lion that is stalking you. *Zambia*

What eats you is not the darkness
but those who travel in the darkness. (Hyenas) *Zambia*

The end of the world is death. *Congo*

Dying is a lonely business.	*Swahili*
It is useless to be afraid of death.	*Yaunde*
Death is like a spoilt child: he gets everything.	*Dama*
Ask the dead man what the grave is like.	*Swahili*
Only the rich fear Death.	*Sudan*
Even the best boat will one day sink.	*Bambara*
Death never comes twice.	*Sudan*
Death shakes us off like the wind shakes the leaves from the trees.	*Kimbundu*
Death, once arrived, does not go away.	*Sudan*
Dying is a man's most frightening experience.	*N. Africa, Swahili*
The dead do not come back.	*Sudan*
Man is looking for wealth while Death is looking for him.	*Kimbundu*
Eat and drink as long as you live, in the grave there is nothing.	*Sudan.*
When the lion is dying, the cow will low at him.	*Kunama*
Lion kills antelope, wolf kills sheep but man kills man.	*Kunama*

As shameless as the killer of babies (i.e. Death).   *Buganda*

The sick man should not pause for a rest on the
cemetery.   *Mali*

A mouse must not look into the cat's game-bag:
he would see his mother's head.   *Ewe*

Only death is just.   *South Africa*

The mantis is watching the butterfly. The shrike
is watching the mantis.   *Botswana*

A dead body will not refuse to decay.   *Tetela*

DEBT

The debtor will not visit the house until his
creditor has died.   *Zande*

The debt is the debtor's joy and the creditor's
worry.   *Yoruba;*
                                            Kimbundu

Borrowing is sweet, bitter is the day of
payment.   *Hausa*

A debt can only be paid with a bigger debt. *Tanzania*

A promise is a debt.   *Swahili*

The rule for debts is to pay for them.   *Swahili*

Lend money and buy an enemy.   *South Africa*

Borrowing brings you poverty.   *Tetela*

The spider lives under a stone.   *Ewe*
(To hide from its creditors.)

Pay your debts or else you will get poorer yet. *South Africa*

The money lender will once have been paid off,
but the tax collector will never be satisfied. *Egypt*

Pay today. Tomorrow may be the day of
Reckoning.   *Swahili*

Forgive your debtors in the hope that God may
forgive you.   *Morocco*

A man who often had to borrow an axe, will
not lend it to anyone once he can afford his
own.

The basket of flour given at the birth of a child
will go back before it is big. (As a return gift.) *Burundi*

If the orphan is in debt, he can only pay
himself.   *Zambia*
(Become a slave.)

The rich man and the poor man cannot agree.   *Congo*

To spend an orphan's money for oneself is
borrowing money from God.   *Sudan*

Do not talk loudly when your pocket is empty.
Your creditors might remember you.   *Congo*

The rich man has many friends.
The borrower has none.   *Congo*

If you make a donkey work for you, you have
to feed him.   *Swahili*

No one can lend you his heart.   *Mozambique*

You owe your irrigation ditch constant digging.   *Mozambique*
(Friendship has to be kep up by presents.)

DEPENDENCE AND INDEPENDENCE

The quiver hangs from the strap and the strap
hangs on the shoulder.   *Mali*
(We all depend on one another.)

The hernia hangs down from the belly.   *Mali*
(Said of parasites.)

The dog you did not feed will not hear your
call.   *Kongo*

If you cut down the big tree, the small trees will
fall down by themselves.   *Zulu*

If you do not help yourself you will soon be
dead.   *Shona*

The cow that follows the herd does not get lost.   *Umbundu*

"Shall I sit down?" Makes a parasite into a per-
manent dweller.   *Yoruba*

When your neighbour's hut burns,
yours will soon burn too.   *Zambia*

The tortoise's food is eaten by others.
Without quick legs what can he do?   *Zambia*

A dog should never bite its master.   *Zambia*

A friend of the dish has no more value than a
fly.   *Congo*

Say thank you so you may get more.   *Congo*

When father comes back (with food) hunger
ceases.   *Congo*

If the trunk dies, the branches die too.   *Swahili*
(Children cannot exist without parents.)

The tree cannot stand up without its roots.   *Zaire*
(Governments cannot exist without people.)

The traveller needs the hospitality of the
villagers.   *Mozambique*

If you pay your chief a mourning visit he will
remember you when the maize is ripe.   *Burundi*

More than one loaf can be made from one
basket of flour.   *Burundi*
(A rich man should be generous.)

Better your own house than a basket of food.   *Burundi*

We all depend on God who gives us every
breath and keeps us standing upright.   *Swahili*

The one who lives between the mountains and
the sky, whose slave is he?   *Swahili*

ENEMIES

Big birds eat little birds.	*Dama*
One day even evil has to stop. (Said by the victim to his oppressor.)	*Dama*
Tell your haters: God is mightier than they.	*Hausa*
Intimidation is not killing yet. (Said by the victim to show that he is unafraid.)	*Dama*
Do not make many enemies at the same time.	*South Africa*
Doing me a favour is not putting a stone in my bed.	*Dama*
When I hate someone, only killing (him) will satisfy me.	*Dama*
He has a face like a termite hill. (Said of a hard, unmerciful character.)	*Dama*
Don't let your enemies get in the way of your work.	*Hausa*
When you are ready to retaliate, take him in the back. (Your enemy is too strong and wicked to risk a frontal attack.)	*Dama*
Behind the aloe is another aloe. (Aloe *Gorse* woods look like waiting enemies.	*Dama*

Be careful when you see one enemy, there are
helpers behind him.)

If you have enemies never go without your
club.

As soon as you touch a termite heap, the angry
termites will appear, ready to sting.   *Dama*

Can the wolf be the friend of the sheep? Can
the Muslim by the friend of the Kunama?   *Kunama*

If someone hates you that need not prevent you
from getting what you want.   *Hausa*

Some people are like nettles: they sting before
you recognize them.   *Ganda*

Some people are like ants: they look insignifi-
cant but they have a nasty sting.   *Buganda*

The vulture's foot spoils the meat.   *Hausa*

What one hyena does, all hyenas do.   *Dama*

EQUALITY AND DIFFERENCE
BIG AND SMALL
TOUT À SA PLACE

From the bare land out in the open,
to the bare beaten floor inside (six of one . . .) *Hausa*

From the coral reefs onto the surf on the rocks. *Swahili*

A needle cannot lift a stuck hoe from the earth. *Hausa*

A small insect spoils a big nut. *Hausa*

Different village, different people. *Kunama*

The hand of a child does not reach the upper
shelf.
The hand of an elder does not enter the
calabash. *Yoruba*

A child may act as a child.
A man must act as a man. *Yoruba*

All people have to go where even the king goes
on foot. *South Africa*

The rat and the peanut plant have an alliance:
the peanut plant will contribute by giving
peanuts and the rat by eating them. The rat says
it is a fair deal. *Bambara*

The hares have long ears, like the donkeys,
but they will never be equally big. *Bambara*

The chief's son has to collect firewood when
destiny destroys him. *Ethiopia*

The chief's daughter will be sold for a basket of
millet in times of famine. *Acholi*

The ass walking with the lion did not greet the
horse. *Sudan*

A prisoner of war does not boast loudly. *Liberia*

The worker is out in the sunshine, the owner
sits in the shade. *Liberia*

The hippopotamus has to go back to the river
where he came from. *Kenya*

People with shoes forget those without. *Kenya*

He has a suit on. Now he behaves like a white
man. *Angola*

We all sit in one boat. *Malawi*

The servant took a big handful of food;
the dog barked loudly. *Liberia*

The mule grazing with the horses imagines to be
their equal. *Somali*

EXPERIENCE AND COMMONSENSE

The swallow is not burnt by the bushfire.	*Zambia*
An old woman can outwit even the devil.	*Morocco*
The cockroach does not choke in the smoke of the kitchen fire.	*Buganda*
The old bird in his tree has seen good and evil on earth.	*Kunama*
Even an experienced man will try something new.	*Somali*
Who will argue with the fish about the number of teeth in the crocodile's mouth?	*Hausa*
He who does not get lost by night will not get lost by day.	*Hausa*
Does the nose know the flavour of the salt?	*Hausa*
The chameleon treads softly wherever he goes.	*South Africa*
The hoe gets better in the hoeing.	*South Africa*
The old bargepole will always float.	*Swahili*
The man who slept in the house knows where it leaks.	*Swahili*
If your mother has not taught you, life will teach you.	*Swahili*

Don't sit on the horse's nose, no matter how
much you know about horses.   *Bambara*

The rat claims to have the longest experience in
the house, but the real expert is the cockroach
in the granary.   *Mali*

The cripple learns more sense than the healthy
boys.   *Shona*

A grown woman is like a stomach: it never says
what it has eaten.   *Shona*
(Learn to keep your discretion.)

If blackberries make you sick you will not eat
them again.   *Zaire*

The snake may let you pass the first time, but
take care not to pass there again.   *Zaire*

Life is the best school—and the hardest.   *South Africa*

Ask the dead man what the grave is like.   *Swahili*

The able blacksmith will never lack work.   *Mayombe*

FAMILY

Brothers must not quarrel over an acre.	*Masai*
A new brother is like a new house.	*E.A.*
A dispute between brothers does not have to be settled by the chief.	*Masai*
Father is a shady tree.	*Kenya*
A man may be famous in the world and yet small in his own house.	*Dama*
Your eyes and nose will tell you if the house is good.	*Dama*
Only the family knows the secret place in the house	*Kimbundu*
If I had no grass to thatch my cabin I should be soaked by the rain. (If I had no family to support me, I'd be hungry.)	*Kimbundu*
Many wives, many children. Many children, many kinsmen. Many kinsmen, many spears.	*Kunama*
Only a fool hates his family.	*Hausa*
When two hippopotamuses quarrel, don't put your oar in. (Don't mix in a family feud.)	*Buganda*

Brothers are like calabashes: they bump each
other but do not break.   *Buganda*

A cow is born with ears; horns come later as
ornaments.   *Tanzania*
(You cannot live without relatives; friends come
later. Said to someone neglecting his family.)

All the boys of the family pee in one hole.   *Kenya*

Do not sell your sister for an ox.   *South Africa*

A tree cannot stand without roots.   *Mayombe*

The son of an elephant will never be a dwarf.   *Yoruba*

A man's hands are his parents: they feed him.

A man's legs are his brother and sister. On what
else can he rely?   *Yoruba*

The calves follow their mothers. The young
plant grows up near the parent stem. The young
antelope leaps where its mother has leaped.   *Zulu*

FEAR AND COURAGE
PRUDENCE AND IMPRUDENCE

What use is fear? Does it prevent Death?	*Bambara*
Courage is the fruit of the decision in the heart.	*Swahili*
Courageous is he who looks carefully before fleeing.	*Kongo*
Do not try to fight a lion if you are not one yourself.	*Swahili*
You are afraid of a donkey's horns.	*Kunama*
An honest man has no fear.	*Kunama*
Fear the claws of lions and the tongues of women.	*Kunama*
If you chase a little boy to his house and he turns there to face you, you know that his father is there.	*Hausa*
It is the hen with chicks that fears the hawk.	*Hausa*
Don't touch even a sleeping scorpion.	*Hausa*
Caution is no cowardice. The soldier-ant walks with his nippers at the ready.	*Buganda*
After the battle the brave man's children wail for they are orphans but the wives of the coward rejoice for he is still alive.	*Buganda*

Better be shy than die.	*South Africa*
A tall tree catches all the wind.	*South Africa*
The *mamba* is not poked at, it is poked at only in thought.	*South Africa*
The tree may float for years in the river, it will never become a crocodile.	*Bambara*
The slow tortoise is strong.	*Tetela*
Do not buy a rat in a bag.	*Tetela*
If you are a goat, do not go to sleep near the leopard's house.	*Ewe*
A shy man is like a fish in a well: he never comes out.	*Hausa*
The eyes that see the king no longer fear the clerk.	*Hausa*

FOOD AND HUNGER

People will eat what they just said is bad food.	*Buganda*
The man who says 'Come on boys, all yours, dig in', is replete himself.	*Buganda*
The beard dances when food is approaching.	*Burganda*
A man's love goes through his stomach. A woman's love goes through her purse.	*South Africa*
Where there are two dishes, the guests may be choosy. When there is only one, all have to eat it.	*Mali*
You cannot eat the sun.	*Tetela*
The beauty of the maizecob may deceive you.	*Tetela*
Your greed may kill you.	*Tetela*
If you want your dinner, do not insult the cook.	*Swahili*
Hunger will break the sugar cane.	*Sudan*
If the elephant picks it up, he knows that he can swallow it.	*Swahili*
Do you hear the rumbling in your neighbour's stomach?	*Somali*
The cook does not have to be a beautiful woman.	*Shona*

| The hyena gets fat on bones. | *Shona* |

(Said to fussy children; look after the
pennies . . .)

| A worn-out spoon is still a spoon. | *Shona* |

Hunger makes a man sell his daughter for a
basket of millet.   *Acholi*

| The hungry boy eats the fruits with the worms. | *Nigeria* |

| A fruit can be eaten only once. | *Zigula* |

If you don't like the frog because it eats slugs
then you will have no meal.   *Zaire*

If there is honey in the tree, the person who has
an axe will get it.

FRIENDS

If you have friends you will not be alone.	*Yaunde*
A friend has patience with you even when you are angry.	*Swahili*
Do not dance in a thorny field. (Do not make friends with a tricky character.)	*Yaunde*
When your friend dies you suddenly miss him.	*Namibia*
A friend's friend is like a ladder on top of a ladder.	*Hausa*
Crying is useless if you have no friends who will listen.	*Angola*
A poor man has no friends.	*Hausa*
As long as all goes well you don't cry, but one day you will remember you had friends.	*Angola*
Every man likes laughing with his own friends.	*Kongo*
Money is the man: if you have none, no one will love you.	*Hausa*
Those who hate you are more numerous that those who love you.	*Hausa*
Do not travel abroad without a friend.	*Egypt*

The best friends are the old ones.	*Egypt*
Some people are like cowdung. It looks dry but the inside is slippery.	*Buganda*
The friends of our friends are our friends.	*Tetela*
Two drinking friends may break a pot (without anger)	*Mayombe*
The bellows' tube is not afraid of the fire. Said of a devoted friend.)	*Yombe*
A good friend is like a brother.	*Swahili*
The image of friendship is truthfulness.	*Egypt*
The friend who goes surety often has to pay.	*Hausa*

52

GOD

There is no appeal against an act of God.	*Kenya*
God cannot be deceived.	*Zaire*
God will prevent flies from stinging the tailless cow.	*Yoruba*
God gave us the seed of every plant, but we must sow it.	*Zande*
God pours rain even on the sorcerer's garden.	*Hausa*
They say there is a God, but He is often asleep.	*Kunama*
Can you demand blood money from God for killing your father? God has no blood.	*Kunama*
You cannot escape God. You will meet him in foreign lands.	*Namibia*
No one can fight heaven.	*Mozambique*
Only God can create new creatures.	*Ethiopia*
All things are done by God.	*Swahili*
God does not put a brave man to shame.	*Somali*
Planning is man's, doing is God's.	*Yoruba*

God gives you gifts. Do not forget where He
took you from.   *Burundi*

God makes the new day when He wishes.   *Swahili*

Life and Death. God is their Master.   *Congo*

People make plans but God makes decisions.   *Congo*

When God shuts a door for us, he will open
another door.   *Swahili*

God lent us his property here so that we too
should lend what we have to our neighbour.   *Swahili*

You cannot improve on heaven's creation.   *Mozambique*

God keeps your cattle when you are away.   *Burundi*

God gives many things, but only once.   *Burundi*

If God gives something He gives life with it.   *Burundi*

God will not save the man who breaks the ties
of brotherhood and friendship.   *Guinea*

God does not sleep.   *Congo*

GOOD AND EVIL

If you don't fear a bull you must be a bull
yourself.   *Swahili*

It is easy for a man to be good, easy to be
evil . . .   *Malagasy*

Be careful when the crocodile attempts to smile.   *Mozambique*

When you see a fly, it comes from the dirt.   *Tsonga,*
                                                    Transvaal

God has created evil people as well as good
people.   *Swahili*

The limit of the sore is the limit of the matter.   *Hausa*
(Evil has its limits.)

A man is like chilli, you don't know how hot he
is before you have chewed him. (Experience)   *Hausa*

Excessive laughter has evil as its cause.   *Hausa*

Never receive a murderer.   *Mozambique*

Money makes the crooked straight.   *South Africa*

A thief in your village is like a flea in your vest. *Zaire*

The silent river carries you away.   *Tanzania*

Nothing is worse for evil than to be told: go
away!   *Mali*

Three evil men can ruin a country.	*Egypt*
Evil lurks in a dark corner.	*South Africa*
The robber's son grows up in the bush.	*South Africa*
If the natives defecate standing up you too defecate standing up.	*Umbundu, Angola*
Good language is what the old men speak.	*Somali*
The murderer will not allow someone else to walk behind him.	*Yoruba*
An evil omen must be investigated at once.	*Zambia*
Be quiet! Mother will give porridge to the child who does not shout.	*Shona*
If you keep the company of thieves you will become one.	*Congo*
If you want to go robbing, choose a big companion. If you have a problem, consult a wise companion.	*Ethiopia*
A servant who does not obey, a justice who does not make peace, are like braying donkeys.	*Ethiopia*

GOSSIP AND SLANDER

God protect us from the tale-bearer.   *Hausa*

The ear can hear what the mouths say.   *Dama*
(Said by someone who knows he is the subject
of a conversation.)

Slander does not reach beyond the river.   *Hausa*

Gossip is like a disease, once you have caught it
it is hard to get rid of.   *Swahili*

Poison that kills from afar.   *Swahili*

A snake has two tongues.   *Dama,*
(Said about someone who says different things
to   *Swahili*
different people.)

Women talk the whole day without knowing
anything.   *Kunama*

A cow can swing her tail both left and right.   *Dama*
(Said of a person who says different things to
different people.)

She rattles like nuts in an empty calabash.   *Dama*

Seeing for myself is what I want, not through
your peephole.   *Dama*

If you have to pass the slanderer's house, have

57

God's name always on your lips.	*Hausa*
When she is a girl she will use her mouth for kissing, later for gossiping.	*Kunama*
Your wife's tongue can make your friends into enemies.	*Kunama*
If you refuse to live with the slanderer, who *will* you live with?	*Hausa*
The tongue will never get tired even when the teeth fall out.	*Tetela*
You hide your faults behind a wall but you parade your neighbour's faults in the market.	*Tetela*
Good ears hear skilfully.	*Ewe*
If you are not going to eat the pap stop stirring it.	*Hausa*
The child of sin will stick its fingers out of the grave.	*Swahili*

GRATITUDE

Let the ungrateful man wipe his mouth.   *Dama*
(Wiping his mouth he will be reminded of the
food he has received.)

Ingratitude is the worst of sins.   *North Africa*

When he has died they will thank him.   *Zulu*

The ass's gratitude is farting.   *Swahili*

Leave some honey for the honey bird who
guided you.   *Zulu*

The ants do not fly back to the nest that nursed
them.
The dead man's money does not go to the wife
that nursed him.   *Buganda*

Ingratitude is the world's reward.   *South Africa*

The leopard devoured the man who fed him.   *Zulu*

Hardship teaches gratitude.
Be thankful for the light God gives.   *South Africa*

The horse that deserves the oats gets the straw.   *South Africa*

The elephant who lent his ear never got it back.   *Ewe*

We are grateful for the blossoms when we eat
the fruits.   *Shona*

If you love the girl you have to love her mother
too.   *Zaire*

He made you rise to work at dawn.
You will thank him at sunset.   *Zigula*

The fruit tree is treated with respect.   *Zulu*

The greedy monster just belches.   *Zulu*

The right hand ignores the left hand that helped
it.   *Ovambo*

How many cured patients remember their
doctor?   *Egypt*

People are grateful as long as they are eating.   *Buganda*

Thanking your host is like laying in store for
later.   *Zulu*

The nurse who looked after the dying man does
not inherit from him.   *Buganda*

The generous sharer satisfies no one.   *Buganda*

Do we thank the river for its water?
Yet it too may dry up.   *Zulu*

Does the mosquito thank you for your blood?   *Swahili*

If you borrow an axe, return it with some of
the ribs it has cut.   *Zulu*

The Prophet Moses made fresh water come out
of a rock in the desert, but who said thank you?   *North Africa*

GREED AND ABSTINENCE

Would you forfeit Paradise for the satisfaction
of your desires?   *Swahili*

One mouthful of food makes him hungry.   *Lamba*
(Give him an inch . . .)   *Zambia*

One day a hand will hit the mosquito . . .   *Malagasy*
(Bloodthirst will be punished.)

There was once a man who devoured meat
every day. So he became a hyena.   *Kunama*

Greed ends only when it is buried.   *North Africa*

The lion's share is the lot.   *South Africa*

The cat never has meat for sale.   *Ewe*
(He eats it all.)

One bracelet does not rattle.   *Tetela*
(A woman wants more.)

Dew will not fill a well.   *Egypt*
(A big bribe is needed to bribe a bureaucrat.)

The flea's greed caused the louse to be killed.   *Swahili*

Greed for the things of this world will keep the
soul out of Paradise.   *Sudan*

The thief's hand is not ashamed of stealing.   *Kongo*

Big belly is not the only one who eats.   *Ovambo*

The trader who charges too much for his wares
has his neck full of charms.   *Kikuyu*
(He fears the curses of those he cheated.)

"Mum and Dad eat well", said the child
and fell with the meat he tried to steal.   *Buganda*

One who says 'Take what you like', has already
had enough.   *Buganda*

Do not try to get the ants from two anthills at
the same time.   *Buganda*

One day you too will eat this animal, if you live
long enough.   *Zaire*
(Have patience.)

The greed of the tax-collector emptied the land.   *Egypt*
(All the farmers emigrated.)

In the end the conqueror was devoured by his
own greed.   *North Africa*

HAPPINESS AND UNHAPPINESS

When you are unhappy you think you will
never be happy. But the days change. *Yaunde*

When you have a bowl of sweet milk in the
desert, be content. *Dama*

Happiness is to follow the will of God. *Egypt*

Happiness is dancing when the drumming is
good. *South Africa*

The truly contented man comes from God. *Hausa*

What makes some laugh makes others cry. *Bambara*

The heart is a tree. It grows where it wants to. *Hausa*

If you have no happiness at home you will not
find it abroad. *Swahili*

The wise man is content sleeping on the beach. *Swahili*

God creates happiness for each of us. *Morocco*

Other people's misfortune is easy to bear. *Malawi*

The dog's happy dream produces no meat. *Yoruba*

Your friend's happiness is like milk:
keep it clean. *Zigula*

No scar will be like the old skin.   *Yoruba*

Where there are many births
there will also be many burials.   *Kikuyu*

Happiness is talking to your friends.   *Zaire*

The sage contemplates God's glory until God
sends him food from Paradise.   *Algeria*

Wealth is happiness. Poverty is disaster.   *Buganda*

Happiness is a mug of strong beer.   *Kenya*

Happiness is like a young cucumber.
Pick it not too early: it would wilt.   *South Africa*

Sweet taste is never longer than your finger.   *South Africa*

When you are happy you think it will be
forever.   *Swahili*

Better than an elegant (but immodest) woman
from the city is a girl from my own village.   *Ethiopia*

HOME

The owl will hoot at night:
he found no place to sleep. *Yaunde*

The woodpecker is proud of his hole in a tree. *Swahili*

The family at home, the donkey in the thistles. *Ethiopia*

Do not propose to a girl whose home you have
not seen. *Yaunde*

The tortoise is the wisest. He carries his own
home. *Bambara*

The homestead is built by hands.
It can be destroyed by tongues. *Kunama*

A home of your own is worth wagons of gold. *South Africa*

The roof shelters the whole family. *Hausa*

Home is where they bake bread. *South Africa*

Roasting requires the mother. The child forgets
the fire. *Shona*

Every bird thinks its nest is the best. *Congo*

Even the dwarf mouse has a hole of its own. *Ovambo*

The frog does not come out of its pool unless it
has to. *Zulu*

Those who love each other need only a small
place.   *Buganda*

In his homeland an old man feels younger.
In his homeland an honourable man is respected
even if he is poor.   *Ethiopia*

The elephant takes on the colour of the home
he has chosen.   *Ethiopia*
(In the forest the elephant becomes darker, in
the sandy lands lighter.)

The breadwinner is the main pillar of the home.   *Zulu*

Do not let the knife destroy its own home.   *Yoruba*

Travel east, travel west, but at home life is best. *South Africa*

Home is a warm bed for the family.   *South Africa*

Even the tiny ant has a home of his own.   *North Africa*

The cock grows proudly on his own dungheap.   *Zaire*

HOST AND GUEST

When your host eats rats, you too eat rats. (When in Rome . . .)	*Swahili*
If you come in through the guest-door, don't ask any awkward questions about local manners. (The people will tell you what to do.)	*Kimbundu*
You will become as thin as a grasshopper if you don't eat more. (Said to encourage a guest.)	*Zulu*
A guest is like a river: he should not be stagnant.	*Kikuyu*
After a week a guest will be accused of the fire in the house.	*Swahili*
Guests are like leaves: they fall off and make room for others.	*Buganda*
Now that the guest has gone who only came to shelter from the rain, here is the big potato for you, my son.	*Buganda*
A good host does not mind laughter.	*Buganda*
If the guest does not clean the plate he does not honour the meal.	*South Africa*
A guest is like a fish: after three days he is no longer fresh.	*South Africa*

The fish in the river is not told to drink.   *Tanzania*
(Said by a satisfied guest when urged to eat
more.)

If you eat alone you will cough alone.   *Egypt*
(If you never invite guests, no friends will help
you when you are sick.)

The twiner-fig kills the host-tree.   *Hausa*

Seek shelter under a mango tree.   *Swahili*
(It has plenty of fruits and much shade.)

A good host is like the kapok tree, scattering its
seeds by the dozen.   *Hausa*

One kraal does not remove hunger.   *Ovambo*
(One needs many friends.)

THE HUMAN HIERARCHY:
SENIORS, SLAVES AND SERVANTS
OR
Big Boss and Little Boss

We are all the slaves of God.   *Swahili*

A slave does not make himself into a free man.
Can a goat change into a hyena?   *Hausa*

The sky will never come down to earth;
the hill will never come down to the valley.   *Hausa*

When the king commands: weep and fill a
calabash with your tears; if you have only one
eye, begin early.   *Hausa*

The fish in the well must not imagine to be the
river fish.   *Hausa*

The leopard covets the lion's den.   *Hausa*

Mr dog hunts for his own pickings and then also
for his master.   *Buganda*

There is always a boss above the boss.   *South Africa*

A man owns what is in his belly.
The rest may be taken by the chief.   *Shona*

A goat is not a dog and your child is not a
slave.   *Shona*
The poor man's children make the rich man's
children fat.   *Buganda*

Do not put the cow and the ass in one stable. *Ethiopia*

A poor man is like an empty calabash.
The chief will throw it away. *Mozambique*

Lady, if you have a slave girl, she will fetch
your water for you. *Zambia*

When the dog kills an antelope, his master takes
the credit. *Congo*

The neck is not above the ears.
Should the ears stick out above the head? *Congo*

If the dog becomes rich they will say Mr Dog. *South Africa*

The fowl died in the bush. There was no
funeral. *Congo*

The poor man has no time for illness. *Mozambique*
(He has to work.)

The man who has paid tax is not afraid of the
authorities. *Mozambique*

Plenty of hair does not pay the debts. *Mozambique*

When you see the chief, help him with the
milking. *Burundi*

HUNTING AND RAIDING

No bird is worthy risking your life for, if you
have to climb a dangerous tree.   *Yaunde*

The hunter knows the languages of the animals.   *Mozambique*

No one can hunt two birds at the same time.   *Yaunde*

The jackal does not hunt a buffalo.   *Angola*
(Do not tackle what is too big for you.)

The little rock rabbit in your hand is worth
more than the eland cow in the bush.   *Sudan*

The hyena will attack an ass only from behind.   *Kunama*

The wilderness is as free as the air we breathe.   *North Africa*
(So you can go and take what you like there.)

The chameleon is not caught in one colour.   *Buganda*

He that sets only one trap will not eat meat.   *Ganda*

He blew the bugle before warning the hunters.   *Buganda*

God may inspect your trap before you do.   *Tanzania*
(And release the animal that was caught in it.)

The dog cannot catch an elephant for you.   *Togo*

Your eyes will catch no game.   *Tetela*

If you do not leave the village you will eat no
buffalo.   *Mongo*

Two hares do not hide in one shrub.   *Ovambo*

The bird that squeaked was seen.   *South Africa*

Foreign cows too give good milk.   *Sudan*
(So, let's go and raid them.)

Catch a hyena with a stinking bit of meat.   *Hausa*

The one who did not join the hunt killed the
buffalo.   *Buganda*

There is no hunting without luck.   *South Africa*

JEALOUSY

It is good to be alone with a dish full of food.
But only then. *Yaunde*

When you are refused a meal, all you can do is
turn your eyes away. *Dama*

We covet what the Portuguese have in their
shop. *Angola*

Jealousy can change a man into a leopard. *Zaire*

While the rich man watches his cattle, death is
watching him. *Kimbundu*
(Sung by the poor cowherd.)

The miser has to fear the haters. *Kikuyu*

Beautiful women are like banana leaves. There
will always be plenty. *Buganda*
(So don't be jealous, man!)

The eyes of those who will eat look at the cow
being slaughtered, and the eyes of those who
will not eat as well. *Buganda*

If you catch a lot of fish, hide it. *Kenya,*
Congo

Jealousy can kill its victim. *Swahili*

When you are a father of many, people will

envy you: the palm tree grows too tall to cut its
leaves.   *Yoruba*

The hill grumbles that all the rainwater runs
into the valley.   *Yoruba*

While your children are hungry, rats are eating
rice.   *Liberia*

Marry a beauty, marry trouble.   *Liberia*

Jealousy is lost in the bush.   *Burundi*

The handsome Joseph entered, and all the
women looked only at him.   *Egypt*

The mouse inside the bag of peanuts called to
his friend outside it: I am still hungry!   *Congo*

The wise husband lives in peace with four
wives.   *Swahili*

The jealous man loses his flesh by looking at the
fat bellies of others.   *Congo*

LEADERSHIP

A good chief is like a food basket. He keeps the
people together.   *Dama*

A good chief is like the forest: everyone can go
there and get something.   *Tetela*

Two male lions cannot rule together in one
valley.   *Kenya*

The cock rules the chickens by pecking.   *Kenya*

The head cannot go without the body.   *Hausa*

Can a dog become a person?   *Dama*
(A poor man is unfit for leadership.)

A chief is like a well: as soon as it collapses the
people will be thirsty.   *Dama*

The tree cannot live without its branches.   *Namibia*
(The tree is the chief, the branches his subjects.)

When the tree falls, the branches too, fall.   *Swahili*

All authority is borrowed from God.   *Swahili*

When the rain ceases all people lament.   *Kimbundu*
("Rain" is a symbol for a good chief.)

A good chief is like a strong tree with many
branches. People like to sit in its shade.   *Dama*

When the moon is half, the stars are bright.   *Hausa*
("Half" is the symbol of weak leadership.)
If the tree is too small to protect you when you
lean against it, it is too small to hurt you when
it falls on you.   *Yoruba*

Good helmsmen are rare in a storm. The best
navigators are standing on the beach.   *South Africa*
(Back-seat drivers.)

The cat's arbitrariness is better than the rat's
justice.   *Egypt.*

Do you want to keep your workmen, keep your
temper.   *South Africa*

The dog whom you did not feed will not hear
your call.   *Zaire*

LEARNING

You cannot learn all the hunter's tricks in one
day.

Learning is for life, eating is for today.	*Swahili*
The old elephant knows where to find water.	*South Africa*
The pulley rope cuts the wellstone. (Perseverance makes the great scholar.)	*Swahili*
Learn with the left hand while you still have the right one. (Learn while your parents are still alive.)	*Namibia*
What you have seen, you know. What you have not seen, you must believe. (But most young people do not want to believe and so they learn the hard way.)	*Namibia*
Ask the dead man what life in the grave is like.	*Swahili*
If you never offer palmwine to your uncle you will not learn many proverbs.	*Yoruba*
The questioner has good reasons for asking unless he is deaf for the answer.	*Hausa*
Don't let the apprentice leather-worker practise on a leopard skin (the symbol of royalty).	*Ghana*
Learning is like sailing the ocean: no one has ever seen it all.	*Swahili*

Don't teach the swallow to fly.   *Zaire*

Learning is the key to the world.   *Swahili*

Children want to change everything but they
cannot make the old cooking pot stand on two
stones instead of three.   *Ghana*

Can a tortoise learn to walk upright?   *Ghana*

If you learn it while young, you can do it when
old.   *South Africa*

An old man cannot learn a blacksmith's work.   *Mali*

Can an owl become a poet?   *Egypt*

The sun cannot be hidden.   *Egypt*
(Brilliance will shine.)

LIFE AND FATE

Every goat will find its butcher.	*Somali*
You cannot turn the wind, so turn your sail.	*Swahili*
Even a crooked sheep has been created by God.	*Shambala*
Life is like your only spade: once it breaks you will never dig again.	*Malagasy*
Miracles can still be seen.	*South Africa*
In the end a man is alone with his fate.	*Swahili*
Life is "look now"; "look later" belongs to God.	*Somali*
Axe, there is the meat! Meat, there is the fire!	*Hausa*
If you are a mallet, hit! If you are a tentpeg, suffer!	*Berber*
God shares out blessings to all men. If a man had that job only some people would receive blessings.	*Berber*
They all watch the cow being slaughtered: those who will eat it and those who will never eat it. They all watch the crops grow: those who will reap and those who will not.	*Buganda*
If the Earth does not give birth to grass and grain we die.	*Sudan*

One man's death is another man's profit.   *South Africa*

The one who says: "We are sitting nicely here",
is not sitting on the anthole.   *Mali*
(The *nkulé* ants sting viciously.)

Everything that boils will become quiet again.   *Lesotho*

The dead body does not refuse to decay.   *Tetela*

The grass in the buffalo's belly, that is what he
owns.   *Shona*
(The future is uncertain.)

The crocodile lives in a little pool.   *Shona*

Danger lurks in a dark corner.   *South Africa.*

The meal will not be eaten by the one it was
cooked for but by the one for whom it was
destined.   *Swahili*

The law of the fishes: the big ones eat the small
ones.   *Swahili*

LOVE

Love cannot be divided.	*Kenya*
Not all lovely houses are for passing the night.	*Mali*
A person we love always does right.	*Yoruba*
Love is an illness and the loved one is the only medicine.	*Swahili*
Love has to be shown by deed, Love is not words.	*Swahili*
At night he is my companion, in the morning he turns away from me. (Sung by a woman.)	*Dama*
An old flower and a fresh flower both have their good features. (Said to a man, who is looking for a young wife, by his first wife.)	*Dama*
When you are young and loved by all you think no one could hate you.	*Yaunde*
Love is like being possessed by a spirit: lovers are not their own masters.	*Zaire*
Lovers need only a small place together.	*Buganda*
Lovers are like two turtledoves, always feeding each other.	*Swahili*

(Love is expressed by constant care and
attention.)

Not all fields are good for cultivation.   *Bambara*
(Not all women are "good" for lovemaking.)

The beautiful fruit that no one has picked: there
must be a hole in it.   *Bambara*
(There must be something wrong with that
unmarried woman.)

Do not beat the mother if you love the child.   *Tetela*

We know whom we love but not those who
love us.   *Yoruba*

Fishes swim towards those of the same size.   *Yoruba*

Love is like seed: it does not choose the ground
on which it falls.   *Zulu*

The finger must go to the cream.   *Zulu*
(The lover must join his sweetheart.)

LUCK (Good and bad)

The lucky man will think his fortune is forever.
The days will change.   *Yaunde*

When you have luck, hold it firmly in your
hand and take it home.   *Swahili*

One day even you will see your lucky star.   *Swahili*

Do not try your luck once. Try it again and
again.   *Zande*

"Unexpected" put an ostrich feather in his hat.   *Dama*
(Only a rich man will buy a hat with an ostrich
feather. A poor boy may have luck and strike it
rich.)

You will meet the cobra when you have no
stick.   *Dama*

Today I do not have it, tomorrow I may get it.   *Dama*

Some people always have a crust left on the bot-
tom of the porridge pan.   *Ewe*

The unlucky animal is between the dog and the
net.   *Tetela*

Luck is a chameleon's skin.   *Togo*

The lucky mouse can hear the cat approaching.   *Dama*

The hyena gobbles on a day of plenty: he may
have to fast for many days after that.   *Bambara*

Your best friend will arrive when the family has
just eaten all the food in the house.   *Dama*

A handful of luck is better than a donkey load
of learning.   *North Africa*

The pot and its lid do not break on one day.   *Tetela*

The nut laughed between the two stones used to
crush it.   *Egypt.*
(Be cheerful even in bad luck.)

When you have, give (so that when you fall on
hard times those you once helped will help
you.)   *Ovambo*

Luck is always just around the corner.   *Buganda*

Do not open your mouth before the food is
there.   *Buganda*
(There is many a slip . . .)

Your bird has flown. Someone else got it.   *Egypt.*

MARRIAGE

No man is complete without marriage.	*Swahili*
The cleared field looks good, the growing crop looks better. (A young bride is lovely, but a wife and mother is even lovelier.)	*Kimbundu*
Marrying is easy but finding money for it is not.	*Hausa*
The criticisms on bride and groom are as numerous as grains in a maizecob.	*Kimbundu*
There is a lid for every pot, a key for every lock.	*Swahili*
The hens are silent when the cock crows.	*Dama*
Your neighbour's wife cannot make you grow up.	*Tetela*
Your chief and your wife: let them talk first.	*Somali*
What makes a girl happier than anything else is her wedding day.	*Kunama*
Beautiful women are like fresh banana leaves: they are picked as soon as they are big enough.	*Buganda*
Married in a hurry: regretted for life.	*South Africa*
It takes two to rub each other's backs.	*Swahili*

Other men can see her beauty, but only her husband knows her faults. *Mali*

If you want to live long with your wife, your heart must be clear (i.e., quiet, patient). *Yombe*

If you marry a widow you have her children as well. *Hausa*

The toad thinks his bride beautiful. *Kongo*

The tortoise marries another tortoise. *Swahili*

A good or bad husband makes little difference, but if the wife is good then all is good. *Kunama*

When father has died, mother will go to sleep near the fire. *Kongo*

Every pot will find its top. *Swahili*

The bigamist dies of hunger. *Buganda*

NAME AND FAME

The worst you can do to a man is to break his
name.   *Swahili*
(Soil his name.)

What does not fly up when you chase it, is not
a bird; what you cannot name is not a human
being.   *Angola*

Your name will live when you have died.   *Swahili*

If the wife is unfaithful, the husband is despised.   *Congo*

The purity of your name is worth more than the
purity of your body.   *Tunisia*

People are like drums: they sound only for the
living king.   *Uganda*
(The dead king's drums remain silent forever.)

Happiness and a good name are fragile things.   *South Africa*

If you have spoilt your name at home, go and
live elsewhere.   *Zaire*

If the father had a good name it will reflect on
the son.   *Zaire*

Even the boys are inventing tales about the
drunkard.   *Namibia*

Even if you wash it, the hand will make itself

dirty. Even if you advise him, the child will
cover himself in disgrace.   *Ethiopia*

That which kills a man will become famous.   *Liberia*

When you have eaten his food you praise his
corpse.   *Liberia*

If the wife steals, the husband loses his name.   *Congo*

Chieftain is a matter of the hand.   *Malawi*
(A chief maintains good relations with presents.)

Married womanhood is mutual hospitality.   *Malawi*

He that has the reputation of being rich,
will have to give presents all his life.   *Zaire*

If you want to be treated with respect, be
polite.   *Zaire*

If you have a praise singer, your fame will
spread.   *Liberia*

The child will be respected if the mother is.   *Zaire*

OLD AGE, SICKNESS AND HEALTH

God knows the medicine for all diseases.	*Swahili*
The path to God is the path to health.	*Swahili*
Suffer or pay the medicine-man.	*Zaire*
Old age cannot be cured.	*Swahili*
Old wagons run a long time.	*South Africa*
In old shoes it is easiest to walk.	*South Africa*
The guinea -fowl does not perch on a corn stalk. (Old persons ought to behave with dignity.)	*Shona*
What I used to eat with my teeth, I now eat with my eyes only.	*Shona*
Do not laugh at your friend's sick child. Tomorrow it will be yours.	*Ovambo*
Good health does not spread, disease does.	*Zulu*
Sickness comes on a swift horse and leaves on a slow donkey.	*South Africa*
Old age is like weeds: they come slowly but will one day cover the whole field.	*Zigula*
Good health is worth all your money.	*South Africa*

Be grateful for old age: God kept you long.	*Swahili*
You mock the old. Soon you will be among them.	*Yoruba*
Where there is sickness, there is death.	*Liberia*
Baldness should be respected, and white hair too, shines.	*Liberia*
Wisdom comes with old age.	*Congo, South Africa*
While you have teeth, crack nuts. (While you are young, enjoy life.)	*Congo*
Old banana stumps rot away to make room for new ones.	*Uganda*
When the lion is sick, the mosquito will come and suck his blood.	*Uganda*
Old people can tell the best tales.	*Swahili*
Ask the aged about good proverbs.	*Nigeria*
Old hunters do not fall into traps.	*South Africa.*

PARENTS

Every man has only one mother. You can share
a mother but not a wife.   *E.A.*

Mother is a field of sweet potatoes.   *North Africa*

A child with parents remains a child. An orphan
will soon be an adult.   *Dama*
(An orphan has to fend for himself.)

If you are strict with your children you will be
respected.   *Ghana*

The pigeon is always feeding its children but she
needs food herself, too.   *Dama*

Even a witch is sad when her child dies.   *Ghana*

You do not know that you love your parents
until they die.   *Dama*

Even a spirit looks after his child.   *Ghana*

No son is better than your own.   *Bambara*

Can you make some other woman your mother?   *Ghana*

A child who has a mother eats twice a day.   *Zulu*
(An orphan eats only once a day, at best.)

Father's advice is like salt in your food.   *Ghana*

No man will starve in his mother's house. *Liberia*

Do you give your child the breast only when it
cries? *Ghana*

The dog's owner can take the bone from its
mouth. *Liberia*

When your child speaks badly, tell him so. Do *Ghana*
not *Ghana* say: "Speak as you wish". *Swahili*

If you threaten to punish your child, do it, or
else he will not respect you. *Ghana*

The son of an elephant cannot be a dwarf. *Yoruba*

The elephant's tusks are not too heavy for him. *Swahili*

The son of a good hunting dog had no sense of
smell. *Ganda*

The earth gave birth to a tree. The tree rose up
into the sky. Then the earth caught the tree by
his feet, saying: "The child belongs to his
mother." *Kunama*

A mother will not reject her child even if it is a
cripple. *Tetela*

If you have no mother you will have to call a
woman mother. *Hausa*

The son of a fool will not become a chief. *Kunama*

PATIENCE AND IMPATIENCE

The patient man eats ripe fruits.	*Swahili*
Patience is the key to all the good things.	*Morocco*
Slowly, slowly the tortoise arrives.	*Swahili*
Be patient! Your boiling pot will not cook any meat.	*Hausa*
The impatient man eats raw food.	*Tanzania*
The slow climber does not fall.	*Somali*
Even God has patience with people.	*Swahili*
A little worm may eat a big tree.	*Dama*
The hasty hyena will choke in the skin.	*Zulu*
Can you carry a red-hot axe blade?	*Hausa*
He often came to watch the mushroom grow, so he can pick it just when it is ripe.	*Buganda*
Be sure to be on the dance-place before the drum begins.	*Buganda*
The one who lies in ambush long enough is assured of catching juicy meat.	*Buganda*

Hurry, hurry, stumble, break a leg, and the

morning will find you in the same place. *Bambara*

As the sun is setting and you run with your
basket of maize to be home before dark, you
will drop your basket and before you can pick
up the maize, it will be dawn and the birds will
help you. *Bambara*

The slow tortoise is strong. *Tetela*

If you want to live long with your wife you
need a quiet heart. *Mayombe*

The Hare says: "Walking slowly leads to death".
The Chameleon says: "Walking quickly leads to
death". *Ewe*

A bull is born with ears. Horns grow later. *Tanzania*

Slowly, slowly cooks the porridge. *Buganda*

PEOPLE
PEOPLE ARE ONLY PEOPLE
(South Africa)

Handsome people are like dogs with big eyes:
some turn out to be good hunting dogs, others
are just thieves.   *Uganda*
(You cannot judge a person's face, even if it's
good-looking.)

People are like ants. They never die out.   *Uganda*

People are like dogs: they always want more.   *Zambia*

People will never agree but rain will make them
all run for shelter.   *Uganda*
('Rain' is the image of a strong leader.)

Every heart knows its own suffering.   *South Africa*

Take care that you don't make the wolf your
shepherd.   *South Africa*

Some people are just chopped into shape with a
blunt axe, but unplaned.   *South Africa*

People are like *mivule* trees, they drop their
leaves and grow new ones.   *Uganda*

Do you believe people who say they have eaten
bitter honey and drunk black milk?   *Ethiopia*

A laughing penis cannot enter.   *Liberia*

A friend is the one who praises you when you
are not there.   *Yoruba*

One's character becomes known only to long
time acquaintances.   *Yoruba*

Watch people's actions.
Do not listen to their words.   *Swahili*

Some people are as hospitable as a thorn-bush
and some guests are more persistent than
bindweed.   *Hausa*

If you want a rest, choose a big tree to sit
under.   *Hausa*
(If you need protection, choose a wealthy man.)

A broad roof has to be well-thatched.   *Hausa*
(If you want to be a popular politician, you
have to give hospitality generously.)

If you have something, people will beat you.   *Liberia*

If you have nothing, try to please people.   *Liberia*

The big fish that eats its mate will become fat. *Lamba*

POVERTY

The eye may see food, the mouth must miss it.	*Dama*
When you visit a poor man you will depart hungry.	*Dama*
Even a man with lean buttocks has a right to his loin cloth.	*Hausa*
A poor man will never throw away an old stick.	*Dama*
Fatmouth, give a piece to greymouth!	*Dama*
A poor man is like an empty calabash. (Calabashes are used to store milk, a sign of wealth.)	*Dama*
Borrowing brings poverty.	*Tetela*
The camel will always urinate backwards. (The poor man will never make progress.)	*North Africa*
A rock will never grow grass but every man has some value.	*Kimbundu*
If you have nothing you are anxious to please.	*Liberia*
"Nobody loves me here", said the beggar when they had not given him a whole new suit of clothes.	*Buganda*
Poverty makes people angry.	*Togo*

A good blacksmith will never be hungry.	*Tetela*
Even a blind cat will still want to hunt mice.	*Egypt*
Even if your mother is poor, she is still your mother.	*Ovambo*
If your mother does not have it, your neighbour's mother will not have it either.	*Kwanyama*
Be patient, donkey, until the clover sprouts.	*Egypt*
If you own only a loincloth, what will you wear when it needs washing?	*Swahili*
Unless you pay your debts you will be poor.	*South Africa*
Bad times are caused by bad men.	*Egypt*
You may cry but your mother will never come back to feed you.	*Ovambo*
The poor man's boat sinks.	*Swahili*
The poor man's hens will not lay and if he has a goat it will die.	*Swahili*

POWER AND POWERLESSNESS

Power does not cross the river (i.e. the frontier). *Mozambique*

The powerful man is always right, even when
he is wrong. *Bambara*

The chicken is not asked if it wants to travel:
its two feet are tied, away it goes. *Bambara*

When the leopard is away the bushcat is king. *Ewe*

Do not come close to the police. They are like a
log with red ants in it. *Zimbabwe*

If you accuse the chief you will soon be in
trouble. *Zambia*

You cannot take medicine for someone else. *Tanzania*

The cow that has died will have no more calves. *Tanzania*

Frowning frogs cannot stop the cows drinking
from the pool. *Kikuyu*

The frog lives in the well and yet people take
water from it. *Swahili*

You cannot stop cows from licking salt. *Uganda*

A nervous dog cannot stop barking. *Kenya*

The housemother may fart noisily. *Liberia*

When the crocodile smiles, be extra careful.   *Swahili*

Authority has no sweetness.   *Mozambique*
(The authorities are never nice.)

You will speak with awe of the chief who once
arrested you.   *Zambia*

If you disobey the chief you disobey the state.   *Congo*

The lion does not fear the dog but its master.   *Sudan*

One boat, one captain.
One woman, one husband.   *Congo*

The leopard will always get his share of the
antelope.   *Congo*

The farmer was beaten by the tax-gatherer.
There was no court case.   *Egypt*

This land belongs to me! said the hyena.
The hedgehog said nothing.   *Sudan*

The mountain can only be measured by the
clouds.   *Angola*

Even the crocodile will not attack the buffalo.   *Angola*

The government is like a leech, like ticks on the
cow.   *Tanzania*

The man who eats with a spoon does not
remember that he once ate with his fingers.   *Congo*

QUARREL

Big people do not quarrel over small vegetables,
unless they are tasty.   *Uganda*

If you quarrel remember that even the Queen-
mother does not interrupt the king's flute
player.   *Uganda*

Where there are people there will be
quarrelling.   *Uganda*

Do not quarrel with a rich man.   *South Africa*

After wind-sowing comes storm-mowing.   *South Africa*

When the beer is in the head, wisdom is in the
pot.   *South Africa*

Smoke curls up from beneath every roof.   *Mali*

The death of a marriage can take place in one
day.   *Zambia*

Quarrel and sleep badly.   *Ewe, Togo*

All quarrelling leads to the devil.   *Swahili*

When you sort out the grain it becomes pure.
When you sort out the quarrel it becomes clear.   *Ethiopia*

Where two quarrel, two are guilty.   *South Africa*

When two quarrel, the first to stop is the wisest.	*South Africa*
Burn your mouth and start a quarrel. (Don't say much.)	*Zambia*
Do not enter a family feud.	*Zulu*
Lend money, buy an enemy.	*South Africa*
Every kite may be driven off by another.	*Somali*
The peacemaker receives the blows.	*Yoruba*
The elephants quarrelled and the grass was crushed.	*Swahili*
The face that accuses is seen.	*Zambia*
He slanders the chief, tomorrow he will lie in ropes.	*Zambia*
You smiled when you borrowed, now smile when you have to repay.	*Zambia*
Do not quarrel with the leopard if you have no spear.	*Zaire*
If you are water, don't marry fire. If you are fire, don't marry water.	*Congo*
Where two hippopotamuses quarrel do not put in your oar.	*Uganda*

RANCOUR AND FORGIVING

The axe forgets but the tree cannot forget.	*Zimbabwe*
The coils of the snake leave a knot in the heart. ('Snake' means 'slander, lies')	*Swahili*
It is past for the eye but not for the heart.	*Angola*
A stone may break your hoe; A word may break your heart.	*Angola*
He that treads on your toe will withdraw his foot at once, but he that treads on your heart will never leave you alone.	*Angola*
Forgive your debtors. One day you need His forgiveness.	*Swahili*
It is easier to forgive than to forget.	*South Africa*
Once you know a vindictive character, avoid him like a snake.	*Swahili*
A woman's anger will last longer than a man's.	*Kenya*
The wound has healed but the heart has not.	*Swahili*
Conciliation is the highest virtue.	*Guinea*
To feed rancour in your heart is worse than suffering poverty.	*Guinea*

Keep your heart pure and without bitterness
with regard to your neighbour. *Guinea*

Can the ant forget that the elephant stepped on
him? *Kenya*

If you never offend anyone your house will not
burn. *Malawi*

Seeking redress in court is like putting your
hand in a hornet's nest. *Malawi*

The one who has a knot in his heart cannot
forgive. *Swahili*

Forgive those who wrong you,
So God may forgive you. *Morocco*

Do not worry over your next meal,
God may have sent it on its way to you already. *Egypt*

SECRETS

The liar has a short life.	*Egypt*
The best way to keep a secret is not to tell it to anyone.	*Swahili*
They eye is a thing that sees. (Said by someone who has seen through his friend's secret but is discreet about it.)	*Dama*
The word that leaves your mouth leaves your control.	*Somali*
A wise man talks about secrets only to his heart.	*Swahili*
Do not wake a sleeping snake.	*South Africa*
The hen with a worm in its bill will not cackle.	*South Africa*
The earth knows who's been buried in it.	*Zaire*
Walls have ears, and little pots too.	*South Africa*
The smoke will give the secret settler away. (To evade taxes and government control, people build their houses in the bush.)	*Tanzania*
If you have a windfall, shut your door and dance unseen.	*South Africa*
If the eye sees not, the heart grieves not.	*Egypt*

You can conceal the illness, but can you hide
the mourners?   *Tanzania*
(You may keep your crime hidden but not the
consequences.)

Obey your tongue and regret it.   *Egypt*

Two wise men will smile, not quarrel.   *Egypt*

If you have sores, wear a clean *kanzu*.   *Swahili*

The giraffe is wise: he never makes a noise but
he can see far away.   *Tanzania*

The virtuous woman sheds silent tears of
jealousy.   *Egypt*

What lies in the heart of a man can only be
known if it passes the throat.   *Yombe*

SELF-INTEREST

The mouth is very large, the eye is very small.	*Ethiopia*
The one who itches is the one who scratches.	*Tanzania*
The one who sleeps in the hut knows where it leaks.	*Swahili*
Each man for himself and God for all of us.	*South Africa*
The tree rejoices when the woodworm dies.	*Shona*
When the worm has killed the tree, the branches too will die. (The children should help their parents in the field.)	*Zigula*
The owner watches the crops better than his servants.	*Yoruba*
The beard joins the hair. (The rich love each other.)	*Buganda*
Those who are provided for think that providing is easy.	*Buganda*
Kinsmen love each other as long as they are all rich.	*Buganda*
The donkey eats thorns with its soft tongue.	*Ethiopia*

In the city he behaves like a citizen.

In the forest he behaves like a wild animal. *Ethiopia*

Stay near the tree so that the fruits may fall on
you. *Swahili*

He milks the cow and the heifer as well. *Zulu*

The tax-collector will even tax snuff boxes. *Zulu*

The dog will try and lie down near the fire. *Zulu*

Family-ties mean nothing for a heartless man. *Yoruba*
There is no god like the throat:
it takes sacrifces daily. *Yoruba*

Giving to one who has given to you
is not giving but paying.
Giving to one who has not given to you
is not giving but throwing away. *Swahili*

They are friends when you have your
beer-party.
They were not friends when your house had to
be built. *Kikuyu*

The cat is always found in the warmest place. *South Africa*

If you are not there, your share is not there
either. *Swahili*

SIN AND GUILT

A frog cannot hide in a dish, his back can be
seen. *Malawi*

A man's urine will always fall near him. *Angola*

The illegitimate child will stick his finger out of
his grave to point at his father. *Swahili*

Inside the fine figtree live the stinging ants. *Malawi*

People are quick to point accusing fingers at
others. *South Africa*
If sin is not punished now, it will be later. *Bambara*

A thing with horns cannot be completely
covered. *Swahili*
(A girl cannot hide her pregnancy.)

Do not beat the dog if you hate his master. *Namibia*

If you have an anus, do not laugh at your
neighbour's farts. *Namibia*

The dark bush smells. *Swahili*
(The dark bush is the adulteress' vagina.)

The son who is too lazy to help his father in the
fields, will starve when his father has worked
himself to death. *Tanzania*

The little dog that licked the meat will be
recognized when it comes back. *Zambia*

One who has sinned does not excuse himself.   *Zambia*

The hunter of the elephant will be killed by the
elephant.   *Congo*

The hyena steals from sheer habit.   *Angola*

Smoke cannot be hidden.   *Burundi*

To replace a lie another is needed.   *Burundi*

Only God can free us from our sins.   *Guinea*

Remove all sinful wishes from your heart and
God will wipe your sins away.   *Guinea*

He that does not do his duty is like a tree
without fruits.   *Guinea*

If you try to hide your guilt, even grass is like a
spy.   *Malawi*

Your half-sister must not be too close to you.   *Malawi*
(Lest you commit incest.)

Your father will come out of his grave to ask
for satisfaction.   *Kenya*

111

SOCIETY

One bad tongue can poison a village.	*Kenya*
Watch your word: it will travel round like a fly from mouth to mouth.	*Zaire*
The back of your head is full of tongues. (People will be polite in your presence, but as soon as you have left they will talk about you.)	*Dama*
A frog who has found his own pool will croak.	*South Africa*
We people are like leaves growing on trees until they are torn off by the wind.	*Dama*
Two mountains will not meet. Two men will meet. (Said to threaten an enemy.)	*Dama*
The lonely man has something to hide.	*Dama*
A timid man eats alone.	*Kongo*
Do you hear the rumbling in your neighbour's stomach? Do your neighbour's sobs keep you from sleeping?	*Burundi*
People are like grass: where you break the earth new grass will grow.	*Buganda*
The nose just wants to breathe. (It wants to mind its own business.)	*Ewe*

If you like yourself, people will like you.	*Ewe*
Have a smile on your lips, even if you have mourning in your heart.	*Tetela*
The crown of virtue is humility.	*Egypt*
Your neighbour is your teacher.	*Egypt*
Few are the good leaders. Numerous are the followers.	*Yoruba*
If you cut off the ties of blood you will have to worry on your own.	*Morocco*
Friendship can neither be bought nor sold.	*Morocco*
All fieldwork is done by relatives together.	*Zulu*
Giving is to make yourself famous.	*Zulu*
People are like ants, creeping over each other's backs.	*Swahili*

SPEECH AND SILENCE

Silence forbodes great turbulence. (A wise man will keep his plans to himself.)	*Swahili*
When the wise man smiles, be careful. (The wise man will not say what you did wrong until you ask him.)	*Dama*
Many words do not fill a basket.	*Yoruba*
The one who talks, thinks, but the one who does not talk thinks more.	*Buganda*
Do not remind the orphan that his parents died.	*Buganda*
Do not touch an old wound.	*South Africa*
Whispering will be followed by hiding, then stealing.	*Kikuyu*
Money and sweet words will open doors.	*South Africa*
A gentleman will sulk in his heart. (He will not show his anger.)	*Swahili*
The silent thief was never found out.	*Zaire*
When he brayed the jackass showed that he was not a lion.	*Egypt*
The talker talks and causes death in his family.	*Haya*

The wisest animal is the giraffe. It never speaks.   *Tanzania*

The talkers will lead the dog to the meat
market.   *Buganda*

A contrary servant is like a braying ass.   *Ethiopia*

The calabash of the ear is never full.   *Zulu*
(The ear is never sated of tales.)

If you tell your friend a secret in the bush and it
becomes known, was it the bush that talked?   *Yoruba*

The much-talker does not know much.   *Zigula*

Clever words may put a man to sleep.   *Zigula*

A gentleman discusses secrets with his own
heart. (Be discreet. Be trustworthy.)   *Swahili*

When a flood comes near, make room for it!
(When a chief speaks, listen quietly.)

All rivers make noise.   *Zulu*
(Where there are people there are quarrels.)

SPIRITS AND WITCHCRAFT

You may kill a hyena in the bush,
a bigger hyena lives in your compound.   *Angola*
("Hyena" is also the symbol for "sorcerer".)

The evil spirit lives with the sorcerer.   *Angola*
(All diseases are reputed to be caused by evil
spirits. These mysterious being are supposed to
hover near the powerful sorcerers and obey
them.)

If two fight over food, the one with witchcraft
always wins.   *Zaire*

Two people quarrelled. It was the sorcerer who
won.   *Zaire*

To tame a spirit, you have to be a stronger
spirit.   *Zimbabwe*

Magic will destroy its master in the end.   *Zulu*

Even a wizard can be hit by a stick.   *Zulu*

One never knows when a witch is present.   *Liberia*

Seeing spirits is not the same as witchcraft.   *Liberia*

Witches will harm you with your own
footprints.   *Liberia*

The sorcerer is successful in everything.   *Zaire*

Witches know each other and warn one another.	*Zambia*
Wife in daytime, hyena at night, that is a witch.	*Zimbabwe*
The death of your child is caused by a witch.	*Zimbabwe*
Living with a wife is like living with a magician.	*Congo*
Witchcraft is caused by jealousy.	*Congo*
A puff adder fills the house. (It is believed to be an ancestral spirit, so many people come to see it.)	*Malawi*
The worshipping of spirits is the worst of sins.	*Swahili*
The witch can be recognized by her daughters' ugly voices.	*Ghana*
Do not count on the protection of other people's ancestor spirits.	*Malawi*
Witchcraft is deceiving the people.	*Swahili*
Not every sorcerer looks severe. (Be extra careful if he looks nice.)	*Swahili*
The sorcerer's zombie dies twice. (An expression of extreme bad luck.)	*Zulu*

SUFFERING AND MISFORTUNE

He died in the bush and was eaten by the
hyenas: double misfortune!   *Swahili*

Tears cannot be seen in pouring rain,
nor can sweat be seen in a dark night.   *Mali*

Tears on a young face will dry up soon.
Ageing eyes have no more tears to shed.   *South Africa*

Vomit beer: friends will help you.
Vomit blood: they will be afraid.   *Mozambique*

The crying of some makes others laugh.   *Mali*

Mother's absence is a great misfortune.   *Mozambique*

Broken arm is carried in a sling.
Broken leg has to use a stick.   *Yombe*
(Small suffering can be alleviated. Extreme suf-
fering is ignored.)

Good luck can be shared with a stranger.
Misfortune can be shared only with your
family.   *Ethiopia*

If the members of a family help one another,
no misfortune will be fatal.   *Ethiopia*

Kindness is the best remedy for suffering.   *Mozambique*

What is misfortune useful for?

A clear space for him who has no space.	*Somali*
All the sages of the land together cannot prevent misfortune.	*Yoruba*
The ox that breaks its leg was the strongest one.	*Kikuyu*
If you die on a journey you will just lie on the road. (Your kinsmen are far away.)	*Liberia*
Hunger throws down even the strong warriors.	*Zambia*
It is a shame and sorrow when you have nothing to give a visiting friend.	*Zambia*
Life will hit you like a stick but what can you do?	*Congo*
No man can evade misfortune.	*Mozambique*
A donkey's work is rewarded with the stick.	*Africa*
When the capital is destroyed, all the citizens lose hope.	*Angola*
The possessions of the invalid will be taken by the healthy. (Double ill luck.)	*Zaire*
God sends misfortune only to purify us. If we are patient, the gate of heaven will open for us.	*Swahili*

TEACHING AND KNOWLEDGE

A hot bit is the cure for a stubborn horse.	*Hausa*
Teaching is the enlightenment of younger brothers.	*Swahili*
A frown does not hurt.	*Hausa*
An unbaked jar is no use for carrying water.	*Hausa*
The boy who was never flogged will not pay attention.	*Hausa*
If your son asks for the knife, give it to him and let him cut himself.	*Swahili*
Learned when young, practised when old.	*South Africa*
Ask the earth what is buried in it.	*East Africa*
Listen carefully and you will learn.	*Kikuyu*
You may believe the flowers when you eat the fruits (kept promises).	*North Africa*
Do not forbid your son to eat hot porridge.	*Tetela*
Knowledge is like an ocean: no man's arms can embrace it.	*Swahili*
If you never offer palmwine to your uncle you will not know many proverbs.	*Yoruba*

If the poet does not teach his song to the people, who will sing it?   *Zanzibar*

The seeker of drunkenness will one day have enough. The seeker of knowledge will never have enough.   *Swahili*

The best talent is a sharp ear and a good memory.   *Kenya*

The size of the cow is known by its hoofprints. The wealth of the owner is known by his housedoor.   *Ovambo*

A fool does not see danger even when warned.   *Ovambo*

Who knows the road to the sky?   *Ovambo*

Without knowledge, if we were not taught we would be like wild animals.   *Swahili*

A wise man is like a boabab tree: no man can clasp his arms around it.   *Ewe*

Ask the dead about the suffering in the grave.   *Swahili*

THIEVES

The surprised dog burned his mouth.   *Dama*
(The greedy dog tried to run away with a piece
of hot meat from the kitchen when he heard
people coming.)

Every thief will have his lucky day.   *Swahili*

The hyena steals out of habit, not because he is
hungry.   *Kimbundu*

A thief too, will find his master one day.   *Swahili*

The hawk lacks no prey and the thief lacks no
malice.   *Angola*

If you go out to steal, bring a companion, so
you can blame him later.   *Kimbundu*

Where there are no rats you can leave your
food baskets on the floor.   *Hausa*

When the owner told the thief to return his property, the thief was indignant.   *Swahili*

Find a thief to catch a thief.   *Swahili*

The opportunity makes the thief.   *South Africa*

The receiver is as wicked as the thief.   *South Africa*

If the vizier deceives you, do not trust the
sultan either.   *Egypt*

If you are hospitable to the Bedouin he will
steal your clothes.   *Egypt*
(Be selective in inviting guests.)

The crocodile does not take the blanket and
leave the owner sleeping.   *Zimbabwe*

If you steal food, eat it in a dark corner.   *Zimbabwe*

The kite steals your chicken. The lecher steals
your wife.   *Swahili*

Big-belly is not the only one who steals food.

The silent beetle eats the seeds.   *Tanzania*

The thief will accuse the owner before he is
himself accused.   *Yoruba*

The thief will make himself into a crocodile so
that he can steal your daughter.   *Zaire*

THOUGHTS IN THE HEART

Thoughts are quicker than gazelles.   *Mali*

Thoughts are free: no one can read them or
steal them.   *South Africa*

Even a child can think. Some do it rather well.   *South Africa*

Only God knows our secret thoughts.   *Swahili*

The heart is full of restless desires.   *Swahili*

Your neighbour's heart is like a forest.   *Tanzania*
(You cannot see what is inside.)

Proverbs are horses for solving problems.   *Yoruba*

When truth is missing, proverbs are used to
discover it.   *Yoruba*

We cannot love that which we do not know.   *Guinea*

Use your head every day. Use medicine only in
time of need.   *Yoruba*

If you do not use your head you will have to
use your legs.   *South Africa*

Wisdom is remembering what you have been
told.   *Zambia*

Some men can build houses in their heads.   *Congo*

(Their brains make them rich.)

Sleep in the house and you will know where it leaks.	*Congo*
Travel on foot, learn the world.	*Zaire*
The eye has never seen enough, the ear has never heard enough.	*Ethiopia*
A man's heart is like the ocean: all the country's rivers cannot fill it.	*Mozambique*
A thought, once written down, does not get lost.	*Guinea*
Unhappy thoughts come from unhappy news.	*Nigeria*
Good thinking is better than good money.	*Mali*
Wisdom is like mushrooms: it comes up late in the season.	*Malawi*
Common sense is enough, leave wisdom to kings.	*Malawi*
The heart has reasons which scholars cannot understand.	*Algeria*
If the farmer grew no crops, the scholar could not study.	*Tanzania*
A thought is like a swallow: it flies away to see what it wants.	*Zaire*
Two thoughts are better than one.	*South Africa*

TIME

God has created Time. Only he is its Master.	*Swahili*
A wise man learns with time, a dog with a stick.	*North Africa*
Who can catch pipesmoke? The ox's blood is lost forever in the sand.	*Bambara*
Time flies. Use it well.	*South Africa*
Can one see the track of a boat on the river? After a while all traces are wiped out.	*Bambara*
No man wins against time.	*South Africa*
How many words of yesterday do you recall?	*Swahili*
Spilled water cannot be picked up.	*Swahili*
Sleep makes all men forget.	*Bambara*
Time teaches many lessons.	*South Africa*
Thoughts are quicker than birds.	*Bambara*
Time makes us all old.	*Kunama*
Patience will overcome suffering.	*Swahili*
The river is rising and you are still eating! (Don't let time run out on you.)	*Buganda*

The old brewer knows the moment of fermenting.	*Nigeria*
Much is gained if time is gained.	*South Africa*
Time cures many wounds.	*South Africa*
Slowly, slowly the tortoise arrives.	*East Africa*
He who lives long has eaten more than the elephant hunter.	*Zaire*
If you had come yesterday you could have eaten honey.	*Ovambo*
If you want to see a lobster sleep you have to wait till the tide is out.	*Yoruba*
The old snake comes out when the sun is warm. (When the time is opportune.)	*Zulu*
When the fig is ripe, pick it.	*Zulu*
The one who goes to see his mushrooms every day can pick them when they are ripe.	*Buganda*
Do not regret the past. As for the future, let no one deceive you.	*Ethiopia*
The meat will not rot in one night.	*Zigula*
The hedgehog finished the long distance slowly.	*Zaire*

TRADE AND TRADES

If you ask too many questions you will not buy.   *Angola*

The trader keeps more than he pays the porters.   *Angola*

When the cat agrees to a partnership with the
mouse, the mouse has to deliver the mice; when
the cat's turn comes, the mouse again has to
deliver mice.   *Bambara*
("The lion's share".)

Leave the handling of the gun to the hunter.   *Angola*

A good tradesman will never go hungry.   *South Africa*

Your neighbour's tools will not do the job for
you.   *Zaire*

Truth cannot be sold on the market palce
but lies are bought with ready cash.   *Yoruba*

God does not favour a lazy trader.   *Yoruba*

You will not have to buy what you find.   *Zimbabwe*

When two honest traders agree, they will both
have profit.   *South Africa*

The cunning trader lives on his tongue.   *South Africa*

When the slave trader preaches the Koran,
farmer watch your daughters.   *Zaire*

A good tailor will sew even on New Year's day.   *Swahili*

The good woodcarver always has a sharp knife.   *Swahili*

The good wine-tapster has many friends.   *Nigeria*

The trader eats before leaving home in the
morning.
There may be nothing where he is going.   *Swahili*

A broken pot empties no boat.
A broken stick kills no snake.   *Zaire*

The trader owes his wealth to his feet.   *Mali*

The basket that was not carried to market was
not sold.   *Zaire*

Spend money first, make profit later.   *South Africa*

The farmer's eye makes the horse fat.   *South Africa*
("The farmer's boot".)

TRAVELLING

When you travel in the rain, you think the
journey will never end.   *Yaunde*

No profit without travelling.   *Nkundo*

Travel with open eyes and you will become a
scholar.   *Swahili*

The jackal knows all the paths of the earth.   *Kunama*

Travelling may bring ill luck for the traveller
abroad as well as for those he left behind.   *Dama*

The bird from afar will be caught by the fowler.   *Yaunde*
(In a foreign land be extra careful.)

A traveller can tell many tales but he cannot
explain all that he has seen.   *Ghana*

The traveller is the one who is on the beach.   *Swahili*
(The one who got up early in the morning will
not miss the boat.)

Travel and study God's world.   *Swahili*

The wind blows where the sailors do not want
to go.   *Swahili*

Travel and hear the prayers of the fishes.   *Swahili*
(See unexpected wonders.)

New things lie in front of moving feet. *Shona*

No one can travel by someone else's star. *Swahili*

Travel light, travel far. *South Africa*

He never marries who never travels. *Zaire*

Find a good companion before starting out. *North Africa*

Only the traveller will see the holy city. *Swahili*

Travel, Swallow, and find food. *Uganda*

Where there is a road, people have passed
before. *Kimbundu*

Pigeon you fly up into the sky, it is Allah who
brings you home. *Hausa*

TRUTH AND LIES

Only in God is there true belief.   *Egypt*

The milk that no one drank yesterday will be
sour now.   *Dama*
(The lies that no one swallowed yesterday will
not go down today either.)

When the jackal reads the scriptures, farmer
watch your hens.   *South Africa*

A plot is always bad unless you're in it.   *Bambara*

Lies are honey at first.   *Somali*

A lonely truth can be brought down by a pack
of lies.   *Mali*

A lie will serve your purpose but once.   *Somali*

Lies have short legs.   *South Africa*

A cow's tail may swing left and right. People's
words may swing left and right.   *Dama*

Only a fool believes everthing he is told.   *Kunama*

Hunger makes the servant praise his master.   *Kunama*

Money cannot talk, yet it can make lies look
true.   *South Africa*

Lying is like putting dirt on your face. *Swahili*

Who knows where to find an honest man? *Swahili*

I carry a jar of palm oil. If you carry a stone
please pass. *Yoruba*
(Palm oil is a symbol for a good reputation
because it is so precious and fragile. Stones are
like slanderous words.)

The persistent slanderer will convince even the
lover of truth. *Mali*

Do not keep a slanderer company. *Kwanyama*

A boaster has few friends. *South Africa*

Fools and infants do not lie. *Kunama*

The dog promised to fetch fire. *Yombe*
(Said when someone is slow or disloyal.)

USEFUL AND USELESS

Do not try to sell finger rings to lepers. *Mali*

The more attempts, the more successes. *Kikuyu*

The motherless child will suck a bitch's tits. *South Africa*

"Almost" cannot be eaten. *Zulu*
(The bird that was almost hit by the arrow, flew
away.)

Do not despise what you have otherwise you
might start stealing. *Zigula*

What is useful? If a cow makes lots of milk and
dung, that is useful. *South Africa*

Even the earth may bcome barren. *Yoruba*

What is useful for the next life is not useful for
this life. *North Africa*

Do not shoot an arrow that may come back to
you. *Somali*

If you cannot reach the hyena with a stick,
abuse will not help either. *Somali*

If you cannot get what you like you will have
to like what you get. *Somali*

Even the sharpest knife-blade cannot carve its
own handle. *Yoruba*

You cannot harvest vegetables quicker than they
grow.   *Ethiopia*

Kindness shown to a hen is not lost.
In course of time it will yield fat gravy.   *Yoruba*

Goats are not bananas.   *Kikuyu*
(Bananas are given away.)

Dried-up water quenches no thirst.   *Kikuyu*

The hare makes a nest wherever he wants to
sleep.   *Zambia*

Leave the eggs. They will turn into birds.
Eggs give no gravy.   *Shona*
(Have patience, and the eggs will produce
chicks, the chicks will become chickens who
will produce gravy.)

Buy what you find.   *Shona*
(You cannot buy what is not for sale.)

Do not try to measure the rivier with your
fingers.   *Congo*

The men who have learnt French only make
more palavers.   *Congo*

The donkey has a soft tongue, yet he can eat
thistles with it.   *Ethiopia.*

VANITY

The sweet potato pushes other plants away
when it grows big.   *Kimbundu*
(A girl who marries thinks herself more impor-
tant than her sisters.)

An important man may be wrong, but he is
always right.   *Bambara*

"I would not have wrecked the ship," said the
man on the beach.   *Swahili*
(Back seat drivers.)

True love is not in the mirror, it is in the heart.   *Swahili*

Beauty is not in bangles, nor is kindness in the
skin.   *South Africa*

To ride a horse is good, to walk on your own
feet is better.   *Bambara*

One bracelet does not tinkle.   *Tetela*

The monkey has a big mouth because, he says,
otherwise he would be too pretty.   *Ewe*

A vulture cannot give you medicine for
baldness.   *Ewe*

He is so clean, a fly would not sit on him.   *Zulu*

The polecat does not know it stinks.   *Zulu*

If the baboon could see his own behind
he would laugh too.   *Kenya*

The elephant does not kill a man whom his own
bravado does not kill.   *Somali*

Butterflies behave like birds but there is no meat
on them.   *Yoruba*

The buffalo said: "If it were not for the
elephant, I would be the biggest in the coun-
try."   *Liberia*

The billy goat emits his smell when entering the
town.   *Liberia*

Do not show your knowledge.
People will call you a sorcerer.   *Congo*

My name is like a song: it is on every man's
lips.
My face is like a mirror: everybody looks at me.   *Congo*

My merits will only be recognized after my
death, spoke the sloth.   *Congo*

The young woman who loves her own beauty:
Let her wait and later look again.   *Egypt*

Young man! You vaunt your strength, but your
ignorance will lead you astray.   *Egypt*

VITALITY, OPTIMISM

The hindmost ox will also reach the kraal.	*South Africa*
The frog does not die in the mud.	*Zaire*
The cockroach does not choke in the smoke.	*Swahili*
Keep your eyes open even when your teeth fall out.	*Namibia*
Old goats love young green leaves.	*South Africa*
I'll have it tomorrow. (Said by someone who has nothing.)	*Namibia*
Eggs break when they fall, people don't. (Said by a man whose adversary has thrown him.)	*Namibia*
An old horse works best.	*Namibia*
People are like plants: they bow down and rise up again.	*Malagasy*
The one in front has arrived, the one behind has only heard about it: go on trying.	*Hausa*
The baobab tree does not die when it falls.	*Swahili*
The chameleon is not caught in one colour.	*Swahili*

The rock rabbit is happy on its rock,

and safe from the lion's attacks.   *South Africa*

People are like *mivule* trees: they shed their old
leaves and grow new ones. (Life has good and
bad periods).   *Buganda*

If the debtor is ill, the creditor will blame him
for habitual laziness.
If his own child is ill, the creditor will spend
money on sacrifices.   *Yoruba*

The old banana leaf dies to give the new shoot
room to grow.   *Zaire*

The palm shoot says it will soon reach the sky.   *Yoruba*

If you have never been sick, you boast of your
strength.   *Liberia*

A lively woman has many friends.   *Liberia*

The swallow is too quick to be caught by the
bushfire.   *Zambia*

The elephant wears his tusks with pride.   *Congo*
(A big family is the parents' pride.)   *Swahili*

The frogs come out of the earth and croak as
soon as it rains on the dead lands.   *Kenya*

Crying a lot does not give you peace of mind.   *Burundi*

WAR AND KILLING

When the Lord created Adam,
spoke the angels: "God forbid
that behind his earthen forehead
he should ever hatch a secret,
covet wealth, invent false untruth,
plan the murder of his brother,
or the savage fire of war
which is worst of all disasters . . ." *The Swahili
Epic of Creation*

Let no man say: "Who murdered my father?"
without his hand on his swordhilt.   *Yoruba*

Many sons many spears, many spears many
raids, many raids many cows.   *Kunama*

A good man loves his friends and kills his
enemies.
Which army wants to fight without a king?   *Swahili*

Terror in the wilderness, shame at home.   *Hausa*

Let the old men fight, said the young man.
Let the young men fight, said the old man.   *Buganda*

War is made by greedy men to prove that might
is right.   *South Africa*

The reed that bends will raise its head
when wind and rain have gone away.   *South Africa*

War does not have one good child. *Ovambo*
Mongo

War has no eyes. *Swahili*

Those who are afraid to wield spears, let them
wield brooms. *Tsonga*

One man you can trust is better than an army of
cowards. *Egypt*

The lion who eats people must be killed. *Zambia*

Even a single cannibal must be got rid of. *Zigula*

A war may start over the theft of one cow. *Kipsigis*

The mother of a coward will not lose all her
sons in war. *Somali*

Waging a war is not like eating a dish of
porridge. *Kikuyu*

Have your war shield ready while you sit. *Zigula*

Starting a war is easy.
Ending it is not. *Egypt*

WATER AND DROUGHT

God has created thirst to try us: bear it with
patience.   *Swahili*

Even a king cannot live without water.   *Bambara*

A stone does not become water.   *Hausa*
(You have to work hard at the well to get
water.)

Even the elders cannot carry a well.   *Bambara*

What is better for the pilgrim at the end of his
journey than cool water?   *Swahili*
(The journey is life itself; the pilgrim is on his
way to meet his Maker; the water is the Well of
the Holy Prophet at the entrance of Paradise.)

The guinea-fowl remains quiet in time of
drought.   *Dama*
*(This rain-loving bird is observed to suffer in
silence.)*

When you are thirsty in the desert, follow the
birds, they will lead you to the water.   *Namibia*

Rain is heaven's greatest blessing.   *Sudan*

God's cup is open.   *Swahili*
(God has created the wells to quench our thirst,
we ought to be grateful to Him for every
draught.)

Without rain no wealth.	*Hausa*
Where there was a pool once there is now only sand. (Everything changes.)	*Sbona*
One does not refuse water to the digger of wells.	*Swabili*
In the dry season grain is not given away.	*Ovambo*
You love your cow in the wet season, you hate her in the dry season (when her milk has dried up).	*Ovambo*
All the men go travelling in the dry season (to find food).	*Ovambo*
Work in the dry season means food in the wet season.	*Ovambo*
There is plenty of water in Paradise.	*North Africa*
Thirst will move nations.	*Sudan*
Rain has no favourites, it falls on every farmer's land.	*Yoruba*

WEALTH

When they say he is generous they mean he is
rich. *Yaunde*
All wealth is given us by God. *Swahili*

Do not buy a stolen cow. You do not know her
former owner. *Namibia*

To be rich is: having a good meal. *Namibia*

The brain is the best store-room for wealth. *Bambara*

You give seed to the farmhand and a cow to the
farmer who knows how to look after her. *Angola*
(Cattle is wealth, to be entrusted only to a man
of class.)

Even after the shaving the sheep has wool left. *Angola*
(A rich man is not easily robbed of *all* his
wealth.)

Porridge sticks to the porridge pan, money
sticks to the wealthy man. *Namibia*

You whose mouth shines with gravy, think of
those who eat only onions. *Namibia*

The rich love each other, like the beard joining
the hair. *Buganda*

The miser's wealth will be eaten by the worms
and so will he. *Swahili*

If you have only a stick in the fire it will be
ashes the next morning, but if you have a big
log it will burn all night for you.   *Hausa*

The rich man mocks the poor man.   *Uganda*

The hare must not try to become the elephant's
travelling companion.   *Bambara*

Shame spent my wealth: I did not dare refuse.
(Said of a generous man.)

The hawk has his eyes on his prey even when
he dies.   *Egypt*
(Said of a tax collector.)

WORK

The slowest camel in the caravan sets the pace.	*Somali*
The cure for poverty is work.	*Yoruba*
The field will yield its fruits when you are tired. (Keep trying.)	*Shona*
If you are healthy, ask for work. (Do not loiter.)	*Zigula*
The animal without a sickle cried during the harvest.	*Zaire*
Where there are fruit trees there live industrious people.	*Swahili*
Sleeping, sleeping, youth is past.	*Zaire*
A lazy man will wait till easy work comes his way.	*Yoruba*
You never carved the bark of a palm tree and you expect to drink palm wine? Does the juice come without labour?	*Yoruba*
Idleness is where the devil finds work.	*South Africa*
That lazy foreman? The boss is his best friend.	*South Africa*
The squirrel starts work in the dew.	*Kikuyu*

When the workers are working they are serious.   *Liberia*

While the sun shines, get firewood for the
night.   *Zambia*

Shivering makes you go out to cut firewood.   *Zambia*

A poor fire makes long cooking.   *Zambia*

If you sleep, your shop too will sleep.   *Kenya*

If you are not there (to work), your share (of
the harvest) will not be there either.   *Kenya*

The sleeping fox: no hare fell into his mouth.   *Congo*

Where there are many fields many farmers have
work. Where there are many people, many
teachers have work.   *Mozambique*

The roof rests on the builders.   *Mozambique*
(Constant attention and mending keeps it up.)

The fire burns because of the wood-gatherers.   *Mozambique*

Hands are worms: they will rot if they do not
work.   *Mozambique*

WORRY

Some people cry hot tears over things they do
not own. *Buganda*

Don't worry about what does not concern you. *Buganda*

Do not worry about tomorrow. *South Africa*

Man often suffers most from the suffering he
fears. Thus he has more suffering than God has
given him. *South Africa*

God rained sadness and worry into man's heart,
but also joy and gladness, but most worry. *Egypt*

The flea in your clothes sets your skin on fire.
(A criminal living near you will keep you worried all the time.) *Zaire*

The past cannot be changed nor can the future
be known. *Swahili*

Sheep and goats will stampede for no reason,
but they will limp for a reason. *Somali*

When your friend is worried, you too feel
depressed. *Liberia*

The first born is a source of worry. *Zambia*

In the beginning a marriage is sugar, in the mid-
dle it is acid, in the end it is bitterness. *Congo*

Men of books make problems that were not
there: big books make big worries.   *Congo*

When their ship sinks, then even the white men
will cry.   *Angola*
(A man will cry when he loses his wife.)

The heart is worried about the many things to
which it is attached. The bird's desire for a few
grains makes it enter the cage.   *Algeria*

Many people suffer most the suffering they fear. *South Africa*

There is no problem that God will not solve.   *Morocco*

Think about your sins and God may forgive
you.   *Guinea*

SWAHILI PROVERBS

Wearing tusks is no trouble for the elephant.

Love is like an illness and the loved one is the only medicine.

When your son is born, start building a house for him.

Lovers are like two turtle doves, always feeding each other.

Porridge sticks to the porridge pan,
Money sticks to the wealthy man.

Travel with open eyes and you will become a scholar.

He that is on the beach before sunrise,
Will get a boat and travel.

When you see dhows sailing, remember how hard it was to build them.

A blind man should not pick up a stick: it might be a snake.

The man who gave up did not become rich.

A girl on her own is like a hen in the field: soon a kite will swoop and pick her up.

A man alone cannot push a dhow into the sea.

The miser's money will be eaten by the cockroaches.

The woodpecker is proud of his hole in a tree.

Without children the world would come to an end.
Without children the house would be silent.

The eye makes the heart desire.
The heart makes the eye look.

Strong teeth can break the sugar cane.

If you want dinner, do not insult the cook.

If the elephant picks it up he knows that he can swallow it.

If the baboon could see his own behind he would laugh too.

Potter! Knead your clay while it is wet.

The seeker of drunkenness will one day have enough.
The seeker of knowledge will never have enough.